Break The Poverty Curse: Unlock Your Prosperity

2017 Edition

Vaughn Berkeley, MBA

BESTSELLING AUTHOR

This book belongs to

_____

_____

_____

_____

A Special Note

_____

_____

_____

_____

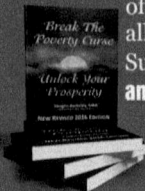

Copyrights & Digital License

The purpose of this book and this series is to educate. It is sold with the understanding that the publisher and author shall have neither liability nor responsibility for any injury caused or alleged to be caused directly or indirectly by the information contained within this book. Where every effort has been made to ensure accuracy, the book's contents should not be construed as a substitute for qualified advice.

Each person's spiritual condition is unique. Seek truth, seek a qualified professional to help guide you, but always follow your heart.

Publisher:
CM BERKELEY MEDIA GROUP
Ontario, Canada
cmberkeleymediagroup.com
Newly Revised 2017 Edition

Print ISBN: 978-1-927820-23-0
Digital ISBN: 978-1-927820-24-7

Copyright

Digital Edition License Notes

Found a typo: Earth is not perfect, and neither are we. If you find a typo, please let us know at http://breakthepovertycurse.com

Books From Vaughn Berkeley

Fresh Food4Life™: The Case For Taking Back Control of Your Food and Empowering Your Family and Community.
This next volume in the series takes a look at the most fundamental right of human beings on the planet. It is the right to have access to good quality food to eat and live. Available in Print and Digital at Amazon worldwide and other retailers.

Bringing Your Heart Home: The Harmonious Approach To Housing Yourself and Your Family
This book is for anyone frustrated with the exorbitant housing prices. It has become obscene what they are selling houses for. Yet we claim that housing is a basic human right. This book unveils the system behind modern housing and why you need to think tiny for your housing needs. Available on Amazon worldwide and other retailers.

Break The Poverty Curse: Unlock Your Prosperity (New Revised 2017 Edition)
This book is for the believer and non-believer who desires to learn about the eternal spiritual principles of prosperity and curses. Universal rules like the force of gravity are always at work in the lives of humans. Without knowing them, you are at risk of bumping into them. This book will help you learn sound principles and doctrine to apply to your journey of freedom from the poverty curse.

The Book on Quantum™ Personal Branding (Coming 2017)
What's the difference between a Tom Cruise, a Richard Branson, and a person like you? They have a brand while you are invisible. Having your personal brand can influence whether you are considered for that new high level job opening, or passed over for a bonus. It influences whether people want to be your friend or just ignore you. Vaughn's book is based on his years of brand building and he shares

insights that is paramount to your personal brand. Vaughn is the creator of The book on Quantum(TM) series of books.

The Book on Quantum™ Leadership (Coming 2017)
There are numerous books on leadership today. Walk into any bookstore and you can be overwhelmed with the choices. What makes this book different? Vaughn approaches leadership from your inner soul outward to the manifestation of your heart desires. There are bad leaders who read the wrong books and use their power to abuse others. Good leaders shape, mold, strengthen, and build. Sometimes it's tough love, but it is always based on love. That's The Book on Quantum Leadership!

The Book on Quantum™ Marriages (Coming 2018)
A good marriage doesn't happen by luck or chance. It's not a flip of the coin. A good marriage is built on godly principles that form the spiritual contract between husband and wife. After that, you've still got to live together, right? Too many people today are ill-prepared for the duties and responsibilities of marriage. Whether you are getting married, already married, or thinking of marriage, you must read this book. This book looks at the recipe for a fabulous marriage. That's The Book on Quantum Marriages!

The Book on Quantum™ Intimacy (Coming 2018)
Intimacy is the secret sauce that explodes your recipe. But what is intimacy? Is it sex? Is it a forbidden glance? Is it a lingering touch? To remove doubts and establish a baseline, you need this book. This book explores the depth of intimacy till it hurts good. That's The Book on Quantum Intimacy!

To learn more about upcoming books in The Book on Quantum™ Series visit the website,
http://thebookonquantum.com

* * * * *

Forget the hype about writing your book in 3 hours, or 1 day, or even one week. You know that quality takes times, don't you? Learn our system to becoming a published author in 90 days? CM Berkeley Media Group has an online training program to help anyone aspiring to achieve this dream. As of 2016, our course is now offered exclusively through the Berkeley Academy! Find out more about it at http://berkeley.academy

* * * * *

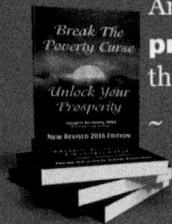

Are you looking for WISDOM?

And God gave Solomon wisdom and understanding exceeding much, and largeness of heart, even as the sand that is on the sea shore. And Solomon's wisdom excelled the wisdom of all the children of the east country, and all the wisdom of Egypt... And he spake three thousand proverbs: and his songs were a thousand and five.

~ 1 Kings 4:29, 30, 32

breakthepovertycurse.com

Book A Workshop

How would you like Vaughn to conduct a Breaking The Poverty Curse workshop at your church, or small group, or university campus club? Yes, it is possible. Vaughn loves sharing God's principles on breaking the poverty curse.

Results of Post Workshop Survey

50% *Attendees felt that they are* now able to *talk about money* and *Breaking The Poverty Curse after the workshop.*

62% Attendees gained a better understanding of the topic after completing the Break The Poverty Workshop!

100% Attendees of the Break The Poverty Curse workshop want Vaughn speak again on the topic and would be willing to tell others about it.

Additional Observations/Feedback From Workshop

- WANTED: The implementation of the community aspect of the presentation with a group of 10 or more committed individuals.
- WANTED: Another workshop/session on how to become an entrepreneur or gain entrepreneurial skills according to heaven's principles.
- WANTED: A copy of the book in order to begin studying the principles in there immediately.
- FEEDBACK: Felt God was speaking to them to get off their behind and give it [Entrepreneurship] a try.
- WANTED: System regarding the aspect of purchasing land and growing their own food as a means of long term prosperity.

Complete the booking form to get Vaughn out as soon as possible so your group can start implementing these good principles today!

Go to **cmberkeleymediagroup.com/bookaworkshop**

* * * * *

Break The Poverty Curse - GEAR!

Great gear for Breaking The Poverty Curse Warriors! What you put in your life influences you! Our gear tells the universe you are Breaking through the spiritual barriers.

Order online at **breakthepovertycurse.com** or through our authorized online retail partner **88deals4u.com**

We have great gear that includes:
- Caps, mugs, cellphone cases
- Pouches, towels, pillows
- Artwork, greeting cards
- T-shirts, and more

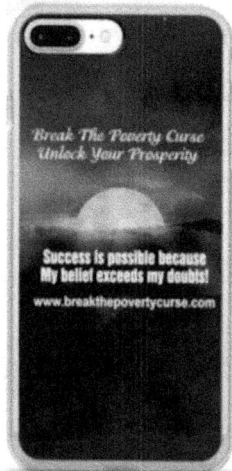

Break The Poverty Curse: DAILY SUCCESS WORKBOOK

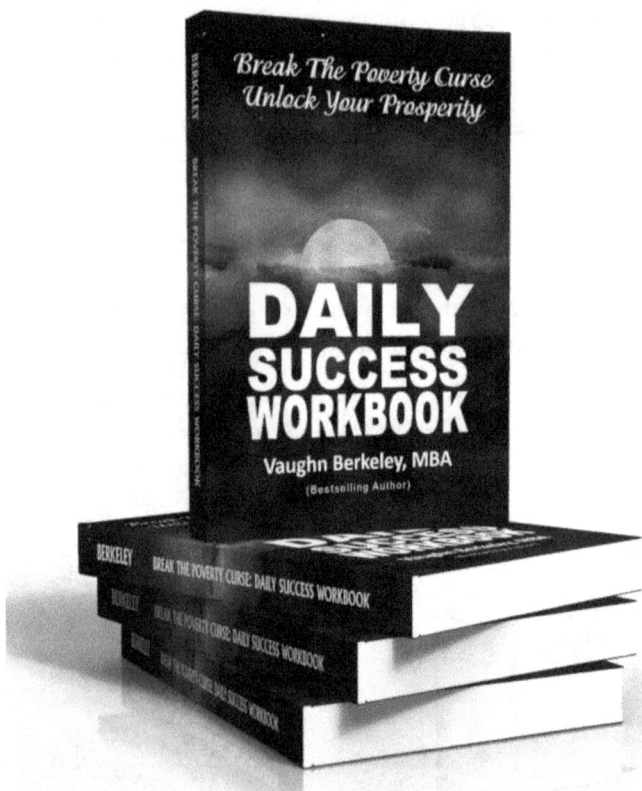

The companion workbook is exactly what you need to focus your attention on attaining heavenly success. Once you start using the workbook along with this book, you'll see why you cannot go back to the old ways of measuring success.

Available at Amazon, Barns and Noble, and online bookstores. You can also find other materials on our website. Breakthepovertycurse.com or 88deals4u.com

* * * * *

Dedication

For if you keep silent at this time, relief and deliverance shall arise… from elsewhere… And who knows but that you have come to the kingdom for such a time as this and for this very occasion? Esther 4:14

It has been a burden on my heart to write this new and updated version of this book since 2012. Yet, the Spirit prevented me from putting this piece of work together until God's timing.

I dedicate this book to Hannah, Andrea, Paul, Carmen, Ashton, Joe, and my other dear friends.

I, in a sense, am like the voice of one crying in the wilderness. I'm crying out to my people suffering under the generational curse of poverty.

This book is also dedicated to all those out there who are under the Spiritual CURSE of Poverty and want to be free.

This book was written for you.

* * * * *

Acknowledgements

This book would not have been possible without the hard work and dedication of all those who support the concepts of good health, a cruelty-free world, justice and equity, and love.

Writing the first edition of the book was difficult enough, but writing this newly revised edition of the book has been an inspired labour of love.

Only another seasoned author truly appreciates the effort and the pain. Many writers have remarked that writing is an all-consuming mistress who desires no other competition for her attention. That seems so true at times.

On that note, we express our love and gratitude for all those on our team who keep the ship afloat and all do their parts to make this possible.

Jean Booth, our editor
Jenny Berkeley, my loving wife (kept me fed)
Caleb Berkeley, my oldest son and advance reader
Paul Nison, friend and rockin' street evangelist
My Inner Circle of Advisors, helpful insights
Trusted Colleagues, our advance readers

Thank you, all.

* * * * *

What's New In This Editon

When I started writing the first edition of this book in 2005, I wanted something that spoke to the deeply spiritual need of those around me. People around me were wholly ignorant of the spiritual principles of prosperity. This is not some kind of prosperity gospel like the ones you hear televangelists peddling. I wanted people to understand the basic and common sense principles of attaining wealth along with warnings against the things which bring the curse. When the book was finally completed by the end of 2008 and later published, I felt amazing.

As you can imagine, the first edition was deeply spiritual. You could not read that book unless you had a Bible nearby. This was great in one sense. However, I was getting feedback that people were using my book as a study group tool instead of studying it on their own and following the principles. And sadly, most Bible study groups are just social gatherings where people rarely put into practice the things they learn.

In 2012, I decided that I would have to write an updated edition of this book. You know, man makes plans but God directs your steps. It seemed that God(Yahweh) did not want me to write the new edition at that time. Thus a revised edition of this book was placed on the back burner until God impressed my heart to go full steam into it.

Why this book? In a world of over 7 billion people, there are hundreds of millions of poor people across the world. They are living in ignorance of the divine principles of prosperity and so find themselves under the poverty curse. Even in developed countries like Canada, USA, the UK, and others, there are millions of people living below the poverty line, and under the poverty curse.

2016 was designated as my sabbatical year. I had been planning it since 2015. By Fall of 2015, I was proclaiming to my wife and business partner, my family and close friends, that I'm taking 2016 as my sabbatical year. God(Yahweh) had other plans or maybe His plan was to use my sabbatical year to finally work on this new edition.

So what's new...

These days there are millions of books that promote making money or get rich quick schemes. This book is totally different for all other books on the market. My book brings heavenly principles direct to you to help you see the truth. The bible says, you shall know the truth and the truth shall set you free. It may hurt your eyes, offend your sensibilities, or jolt you. But I pray for you to wake up from the slumber of this world.

Firstly, this new edition has been reorganized and the information ordered in a way which recognizes the human form. You will see the content has been divided into spiritual, mental, and physical categories. I've also envisioned a completely new money strategies category.

There are some totally new concepts and insights which I have acquired over the years that have been added into this new edition, resulting in more chapters than the original book. This book is like a mini-course in micro-economics, macro-economics, finance, business management , and divinity all rolled into one. It is a foundational book aimed at building communities.

There is still a lot of scriptural content because rules of Yahuah (God) are timeless where your personal finances are concerned. He has stated in the Holy Scriptures that He gives power to get wealth.

There are more options for meditating and reflecting on the concepts. There are also more spaces to write in your comments and thoughts as you study bible verses. I want this to be your book and when you write in it, you personalize it to you.

It starts with a dream…

I have a dream on my heart for this book. I want to have 1 million of copies of this book in the hands of readers who will take action for God. I'd also like to donate copies of the book to women's shelters, half-way homes, orphanages, and prisons. With the hundreds of millions of people living in poverty and under the CURSE, a million is a drop in the bucket. But it will give those folks a chance to impact their communities and create a ripple effect of love, compassion, and breaking the chains of the poverty curse. You can help me achieve this goal. Pray that God(Yahuah) will make it happen. Buy a copy of the book for your friends and loved ones if you are able. Recommend the book to others. Let's get the word out.

You will see I have used Yahweh or Yahuah in brackets to show the name of God. The word god is a generic title, but the Bible teaches that we shall call upon on the name of our God. Do you know his name? Now you can as you read the book.

This book was also designed to be used as the core textbook for my online course where students can gain more insight from me as I walk though the concepts along with loads of extra information that couldn't fit inside this book. If you're curious about the course, you can check it out at http://berkeley.academy

This book is especially relevant since we are all still hurting from the recent 2009 USA housing bubble crash and the market crash. I wanted to put in some truly practical ideas for the ordinary working man and/or woman who has had enough of bearing the burden of careless men and women in positions of power over finances.

There are 12 pillars of life that rulers attempt to control in order to exercise control of you and the masses. These twelve pillars are:

1) Education - how the population of the future will behave
2) Money - the means of holding wealth
3) Law - the authority to enforce the will of the state
4) Politics - the direction of the state
5) Economy - the creation of wealth
6) History - what people believe happened in the past
7) Psychology - controlling how people think
8) Philanthropy - people think well of their controllers
9) Medicine - the power of health, life, and death
10) Religion - people's spiritual belief
11) Media - what people know and learn about current events
12) Continuity - power to say who follows in your footsteps

In restructuring this book, my sincere hope and prayer is that you will be guided to take control of your financial destiny with both hands and with God (Yahuah)as your guiding light.

This control over your financial destiny affects the pillars of money, economy, and to some extent philanthropy. Thus, these three pillars will be impacted by your study of the godly principles in this book. Additionally, I encourage you to open your eyes to other pillars and seek knowledge in all of these areas for your life and that of your family. God(Yahweh) would have you empowered in all areas of your life so that you prosper, even as your soul prospers.

* * * * *

Our Covenant

Believe it or not, this book was written for you.

It was prepared for this exact moment in time when you held it in your hand. You might have noticed it - a different feeling; something clicked; it just seemed right but you couldn't quite put your finger on it.

Isaiah 1:18-19 says, '18 Come now, and let us reason together, says the Lord. Though your sins are like scarlet, they shall be as white as snow; though they are red like crimson, they shall be like wool. 19 If you are willing and obedient, you shall eat the good of the land'

Nothing happens out of season. And with God(Yahuah), all things occur in the time he has planned. Therefore, you are now reading these words because it was meant to be so. Now you have the chance to make a covenant for your financial future.

With the Almighty's help, I resolve to read this book, commit the precepts to my heart and get out from the CURSE. I further resolve to help others get out of the CURSE without hesitation or delay once I get out from under the CURSE.

_____

Your Name

_____

Date

Vaughn Berkeley
Your Spiritual Witness / Supporter / Guide

Make your covenant online at breakthepovertycurse.com

The Preview Chapter

Are you looking for WISDOM?

For the LORD **giveth wisdom**: out of his mouth **cometh knowledge and understanding.** He layeth up **sound wisdom for the righteous**: he is a buckler to them that <u>walk uprightly</u>.

~ Proverbs 2:6-7

breakthepovertycurse.com

This chapter is the preview chapter. You know like in the movies you get a 1 or 2 minute preview of an upcoming movie. Well, I'm trying to apply that method to this book. Why? Because I want you to understand without a shadow of a doubt why you need to purchase this book.

Let's take a walk through this preview together, shall we.

Imagine, you're working at your job. The boss has asked you to do a project that you are fully capable of doing well. You're secretly overjoyed to get the project but you don't show it too much. You tell yourself that this is a cake walk. It is so easy that you can now show the boss how magnificent and skilful you are. You imagine that soon after you may be able to get that raise that you wanted. You're smiling from ear to ear. You think, this is so great.

As you're working on the project, all the pieces are falling into place. And you're laughing to yourself. Days pass by. It's a big project and you know you will have it completed on time because you have the knowledge, skills, and abilities to get it done.

Suddenly after completing about 70% of the project, things just start to go wrong. At first, it's small things that cause you delay. Then it gets bigger and you are forced to rework things you've already done. You don't understand it. As the days go by more and more bad things keep happening on your project. Now you're getting stressed and anxious. You're feeling the pressure. This cake walk is now turning into a fire walk. You go home at night freaking out about when will it be over. You feel like it is a noose around your neck.

To make matters worst, friends drop comments like, "you must have the worst luck" or "maybe you're just getting some bad karma". A friend or two may try to be helpful and tell you that you should go see the witch doctor, or the pundit, or the priest because you might have some black magic affecting you. Others say it's just bad luck.

Then just when you think you're pulling the project through it fails completely at the deadline. Your boss is upset, your prospects for advancement are ruined. You eventually leave the job because you're not going to be promoted. You ask yourself why. You knew everything. It was supposed to be a piece of cake. Yet it failed.

Now I want you to imagine with me another thing. Imagine you need a small car for yourself. You decide you're going to buy a used car. You talk to your good friend and he agrees to sell you his car cheap. You've ridden in it before and it has never given any problems. Your friend maintains it well so there should be no problems. The car is a bit old but everything seems fine.

You buy the car from your friend and you begin to use it. Everything seems fine for six months. Then suddenly, your car begins to develop all sorts of problems. You go to the mechanic and spend $100 here and there. After a year, the car is costing you a lot to fix. You begin to ask yourself if your friend sold you a worthless piece of junk. But you doubt it because it worked well for him. What could be the problem, you think to yourself. You begin to think that maybe you have the worst luck or you're just bad lucky.

Now imagine with me you're in school working on an assignment. You know it should be easy. You worked hard on it because you want to get good grades. You're proud of what you have accomplished. You feel like you're on top of the world.

Then suddenly, out of nowhere, your assignment flies out of your hand in wind. You're stunned. You start running to try to catch it. It's the only copy, the final copy you have and it will take at least a week to redo it. But the wind does not care. Within minutes, it is gone far out of your reach and eventually out of your sight. You begin to cry and sob because it was a great assignment and now to have to face the shame of not being able to hand it in. You walk to school depressed and full of despair.

Now I want you to think about these stories and think how unfortunate or unlucky they are. If they were you, it would be tremendously heartbreaking. Yet, these kind of things and worst are happening to real human beings all around us.

Sometimes people say that a witchdoctor put a curse on them. Other times someone dabbling in the occult gets the blame for putting a hex, spell or some other act.

But what about people who have had things like this happening in their lives for 2, 3, 5, 7, or 15 years. Their lives seem to be perpetually filled with unlucky experiences. For them, it appears like they are chronically cursed. Their friends become superstitious of them and don't want them involved in something important because they think the bad luck will cause it to fail. It begins to isolate them from people bit by bit.

When you visualized these things in your mind, what you were actually looking at was the outcome or manifestation of the POVERTY Curse. Can this be real?

Yes, the POVERTY CURSE had manifested itself mildly in the lives of some people and as a chronic condition in others. Yet, most people NEVER ever think of their condition as being rooted in a spiritual condition.

It is easier to call it bad luck and dismiss the whole thing. You see, luck, whether good or bad, cannot really be attributed to any deity or entity. It's like a meaningless vapour. So calling something lucky allows you to acknowledge the event in the moment and dismiss it the following moment.

That's the danger of the POVERTY CURSE for believers in God, Yahweh(Yahuah) and Jesus(Yahusha). If they are complacent in their spiritual life, they could unwittingly allow the POVERTY Curse to manifest in their lives. YOU could be doing the things right now that cause it to manifest in your life without you knowing that you are doing the thing which triggers it.

Now think about one more thing for me. Think about two business owners. One business owner is struggling for years. They are just barely making enough money to survive. The other business owner is making tons of cash and drives an expensive car. On the surface, it might seem like one business owner is suffering from the POVERTY CURSE while the other business owner is prosperous. Yet, if you look closer, you might see that the business owner making just enough money to survive has a happy home life, is a god-fearing man, and is kind to others. You might also see the business owner who is making lots of cash being in one unhappy relationship after another. You might also see that at night when they are alone, depression, fear, and panic grips them. He/she sleeps with the lights on because they are afraid at night. Though the business owner has lots of money, they have no peace of mind or quietness of spirit. That business owner is suffering under the POVERTY CURSE. Outwardly things were not as they appeared to be.

The words of Revelation 3:17 state, "Because thou sayest, I am rich, and increased with goods, and have need of

nothing; and knowest not that thou art wretched, and miserable, and poor, and blind, and naked:"
What we see described here could be used to describe the business owner. Though they think they are rich, and increased in goods, yet God (Yahuah) says they are poor, wretched, and naked. They are under the POVERTY CURSE in the spiritual realm.

You may well be doing things to trigger the POVERTY Curse in your own life.

"How can this be?" you ask. Because most people today are woefully ignorant on the topic of spiritual matters. Most people are caught in foolish fables like the tooth fairy, Easter bunnies, and other such nonsense while the real power of spiritual forces are unknown to them and truly known only to a few on both sides of the battle.

Why do the rich get richer while the poor get poorer? There can be multiple reasons on the visible spectrum. The rich have access to cash. They have good deals falling in their laps. They have access to insider information which allows them to profit from it. They exploit the poor in order keep themselves in the money. But there is another reason that most people overlook. Some of the rich use their power and influence to mislead the poor into doing things in their lives which bring the POVERTY Curse into their lives. Thus the rich lead the poor as blind people are led into a ditch. Some of those rich had partnered with demonic spiritual forces in order to secure their wealth at the expense of ignorant poor folks. Can a rich business owner make a deal with a witch or warlock or other demonic entity to have their business grow and become successful? Yes, they can. Can musicians or other entertainers make deals with agents of demons to gain success in their careers? Yes, they can.

Sometimes you hear about it but in all the noise of modern day society, you simply dismiss it. You can hear it in a music lyric or see the symbolism represented in music videos. Those who are wholly ignorant of these signs cannot tell but those with some knowledge know immediately what they mean. Demonic forces have assisted in the monetary success of a few in order to entice the many, with the purpose of destroying all. Demons (fallen angels/exiles of the kingdom of heaven) have a burning hatred of all human beings. Ordinary humans are beneath them in physical strength, in intelligence, and in spiritual power. Using deception, the exiles of the kingdom of heaven appear as benevolent creatures wanting nothing more than to free humans from the shackles of the law of God, Yahweh.

The Bible expressly forbids God's people from engaging in working with demonic forces.

Consider Moses in Egypt with me for a moment. Today we have magicians doing amazing feats of magic like walking through solid objects, turning one object into something else, and other feats. Back in the time of Moses, the wizards and sorcerers were masters of occultist spiritual power. They had full knowledge of partnering with demons, the exiles of the kingdom of heaven.

Consider the story of Moses in Exodus 4:2-4. God (Yahuah) tells Moses to throw his rod on the ground and this rod becomes a living creature. It becomes a live snake. Moses ran from the snake but when God(Yahuah) told him to grab the snake by the tail, it became a rod again in his hand. Later on when Moses with his brother Aaron go to see Pharaoh, they throw the staff down and it becomes a live snake. But instead of Pharaoh being amazed, he calls for his magicians to do the same thing. Those magicians also throw their rods down and their rods turn into living snakes.

The ability to turn an inanimate wooden stick into a living snake is a spiritual power not a natural human ability. Moses was able to turn the rod into a snake by the power of the Almighty God, Yahuah. The magicians were able to turn the rods into snakes by powerful demonic forces working with them. Thus in that moment we see a standoff between the representative of God, Moses, and the representatives of the

exiles of the kingdom of heaven, the magicians. One
righteous against many unrighteous.

However, in Exodus we see something that only happened
with the power of God (Yahuah). Moses' snake swallowed
up all the snakes of the magicians. Then when Moses and
Aaron grabbed their snake by the tail, it became a rod again.
The magicians had no snakes/rods to pick up.

There are spiritual forces at work in the world both for and
against those of us in the world. Yet, the Bible teaches the
just shall live by their faith.

Now I want you to think back over your life. Do you think
that you suffer with too much "bad luck"? Are you living in
a family that has been poor (in relationships, in health, in
finances) for generations and nothing you do seems to lift
you up out of it? Does your life appear like it is just one
frustration after another? Is your family so dysfunctional that
it seems like there could never be true unity?

YOU could be suffering under the POVERTY CURSE. It
could be an acute case or maybe a chronic case. It could have
been on your family for generations and no one has shown
anyone in your family how to break this POVERTY
CURSE.

And so it is now up to you. You are the one in your family
reading this book. Somehow, God (Yahweh) wanted you to
get access to the information in this book. It was not a
coincidence that you got this book. There are no
coincidences for those who live by faith. There is also no
such thing as bad luck or good luck.

You have to make a choice in your life. Do you open up the
box that contains the answers you may be seeking but you
do not want to hear? Do you partake of the meal that seems
sweet to your tongue but seems bitter to your stomach? Do
you go forward in an attempt to Break The POVERTY
CURSE and Unlock Your Prosperity? Or do you run away
and hide and claim that ignorance is bliss?

Choices, choices, you have to make the choice for yourself. The prophet of God (Yahweh), Isaiah, when he had come before the throne in a vision exclaimed, "Woe is me, for I am undone! Because I am a man of unclean lips and I dwell in the midst of a people of unclean lips, for my eyes have seen the king, Yahuah of hosts." Isaiah understood that he lived among a nation where lies and deceit was the norm. It grieved him. And if you are reading this book, I suspect it grieves you too that our society has come to this state.

The rich get richer while the poor get poorer! Why?
Find answers to this question in the book.

You could be bringing curses upon yourself! How?
Find answers to this question in the book.

You might be doing so much and still can't get ahead! Why?
Find answers to this question in the book.

This powerful force keeps poverty ever present. What is it?
Find answers to this question in the book.

Timing is important to effect change and break poverty. When is it?
Find answers to this question in the book.

There is a heavenly system to breaking the curse. What?
Find answers to this question in the book.

Yet, our good God, Yahweh gives us hope. In Isaiah's story, he sent an angel to cleanse Isaiah's unclean lips then he sent Isaiah to be a messenger of the kingdom of heaven.

There are still questions to be answered with respect to the POVERTY Curse.

When I was in school I had some really awesome teachers. The best ones didn't give you the answer to your questions but gave you clues and helped you to discover the truth for yourself.

This book will teach you some of the answers but will also give you the opportunity to search out the truth for yourself. You will be shown where to look to find it and from there you can unearth the truth for yourself.

The questions are important and the answers can change your life.

This book is for those who have faced the battle of life and have come out battered, bruised, broken but not shattered. It is for you if you are now ready to fight for all that is rightfully yours according to the laws of the kingdom of heaven.

Yet, it must be said that one must heed the warning against all those who wish to fight against truth. Those who fight against the truth will experience something comparable to these words of Isaiah in Isaiah 29:8, "It shall even be as when a hungry one dreams; and, behold, he is eating; but when he awakes, his soul is empty. Or it shall be as when a thirsty one dreams; and, behold, he is drinking, but when he awakes, he is faint, and his soul is longing. So shall be the multitude of all the nations who fight against Mount Zion."

You see, beloved, there is a war taking place on planet earth. It is not the war between nation states. It is not the war between factions in the same country. It is a war between two spiritual kingdoms. The one kingdom is the true Kingdom of God (Yahuah) and all the angelic hosts of heaven. The other kingdom is the one set up on earth by the exiles of Kingdom of God, that is, the devil and his fallen angels.

Remember Jesus(Yahusha) said that his kingdom was not of this world. His kingdom was not a physical kingdom of this world like the Jewish kingdom as he was accused of calling himself the king of the Jews. His kingdom was the spiritual Kingdom of Heaven. Jesus(Yahusha) said, if his kingdom were of this world, his subjects would fight for him.

Now look at the second spiritual kingdom. Here are two witnesses to this. Jesus(Yahusha) accused the Jewish leaders of his time of being followers of their father the devil. He said that they do Satan's will and reject the call to repent. The devil himself when tempting Jesus(Yahusha) took him up on a high mountain and showed him all the kingdoms of the world. Then Satan offered to give Jesus(Yahusha) all those kingdoms if Jesus would only bow down (worship) Satan.

Jesus(Yahusha) rebuked Satan as it is recorded in Matthew 4:10, "Then saith Jesus unto him, Get thee hence, Satan: for it is written, Thou shalt worship the Lord(Yahuah) thy God, and him only shalt thou serve."

The POVERTY Curse is meant to impede the progress of those human agents aligned with the kingdom of Satan. Some of the agents in this kingdom succumb to the POVERTY Curse. Others ensnare agents of the Kingdom of Heaven in the POVERTY Curse to destroy them too. It is my hope for you that you would be like those wonderful people who really wanted to know about God, Yahweh, and of his kingdom. In the book of Nehemiah we see in Nehemiah 8:1, "And all the people gathered as one man into the street [plaza of the sanctuary] before the Water Gate.† And they spoke to Ezra the scribe to **bring the Book of the Torah of Moses**, which God [Yahuah] had commanded to Israel."

They wanted to know what was in the book because they wanted something better for their lives. They knew that there were answers to their questions in the book and they were hungry for it. Are you hungry to break the POVERTY Curse in your life?

It seems appropriate to quote John the Baptist here: ***Repent! For the kingdom of Heaven has drawn near.***

May Yahuah bless you as you continue to walk in the truth he reveals in your life.

If you are ready, strap in because it's time to open up the book.

* * * * *

Inspirational Artwork

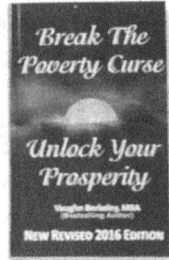

Having beautiful artwork in your home can help to inspire you every day as you look at it. The art must have meaning to it. This beautifully crafted canvass print of the sun emerging from cosmic clouds can be yours. Hang it in your home as a reminder that you are breaking free just as the sun is. This piece was created by Vaughn Berkeley. He fell in love with it and selected it for his book cover. Now you can have this too! Find our how to order it online at http://cmberkeleymediagroup.com/shop or http://88deals4u.com

Contents

* * * * *

The Holistic Health Nurse Series™ Vol 4

FRESH

Food4life™

The Case For Taking Back Control of Your
Food And Empowering Your Family And
Community.

1st Edition

Jenny Berkeley, RN
Best Selling Author
&
Vaughn Berkeley, MBA

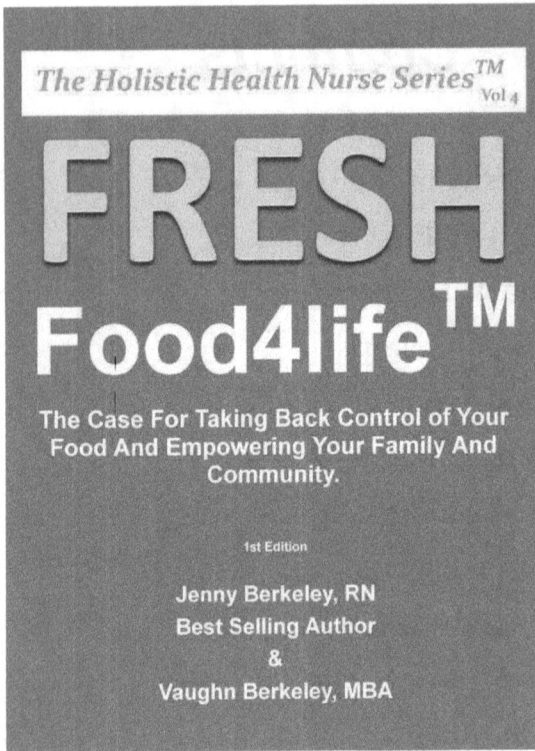

Food is one of the areas that can be
impacted by the Poverty Curse.
Most people are now trapped in our
modern food supply system. Do you
understand how this system works?
Do you know how to empower
yourself and your family with food?
Order this book today!

Vaughn Berkeley, MBA

The Spiritual Dimension

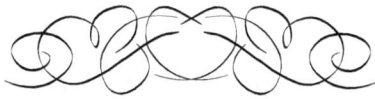

I

The Wise Teacher

In this Spiritual Dimension section of the book, we're going to become familiar with the spiritual aspects of earning prosperity while breaking the Poverty Curse.

The Spirituality of Money

Chapter 1

* * *

A generation ago there were a thousand men to every opportunity… while today there are a thousand opportunities to every man. - Henry Ford

To every thing there is a season, and a time to every purpose under the heaven: A time to be born, and a time to die; a time to plant, and a time to pluck up that which is planted; A time to kill, and a time to heal; a time to break down, and a time to build up; A time to weep, and a time to laugh; a time to mourn, and a time to dance; - Ecclesiastes 3:1-4

Those with a knowledge of money use this knowledge to the detriment of those without such knowledge. It is imperative that ordinary people learn financial wisdom in order to secure their future. ~ Vaughn Berkeley, MBA

* * *

Did you know that the bible contains over 700 references to money? For there to be so many references, it must have been a very important topic for earthlings to ponder. Have you investigated all of them for yourself? Why not? Aren't you curious about what blessings or curses surround those statements about money?

I was curious. I had heard that the love of money is the root of all evil, according to the scriptures. But money itself is a tool used for good or bad. God (Yahweh) allows money for character building. If a person can be trusted in something as small (spiritually insignificant) as money, certainly that person can be trusted with the weightier matters of heaven.

Money is a tool and poverty is a CURSE.

What is Poverty?

When I first began writing this book in 2005, I had not envisioned the crash of 2008. I had, however, noticed that people were becoming more and more ignorant of the timeless principles of good financial stewardship. When I stated, "A tidal wave of poverty is coming," I could not imagine how close we were to the crash. And yet, that 2008 crash was not the BIG one. It was merely a first ripple of what might be on the horizon unless people wake up.

Yes, a tidal wave of poverty is coming which will be like that of the time of Joseph or Nehemiah. The 2008 economic crash of America and the weakening global financial systems worldwide have indeed happened as I had originally predicted in 2005. The middle class people have taken a huge hit as they watched their retirement funds get slashed by 1/4, 1/3, or even 1/2. Others have lost their homes or seen the value drop below what they paid for it.

But more of this is still to come. The middle class are going to be wiped out if they fail to heed the warning. The rich will not be insulated from the CURSE, for their part played in bringing the devastation. Are you going to be consumed?

Here are some good definitions of poverty:
- The state of being poor; lack of the means of providing material needs or comforts.
- Deficiency in amount; scantiness.
- Unproductiveness; infertility.
- The state of having little or no money and few or no material possessions.

All of these together pretty much sum up poverty.

Poverty is, not having the means of providing material needs or comforts. This means not being able to acquire the items you need to make your life and the life of your loved ones worth living or even comfortable. Poverty is also about having a deficiency in amounts and resources. It is about unproductiveness, idleness, and lastly it is having nothing or very little. You see, poverty extends beyond the physical and goes all the way into the spiritual realm as you'll find out by reading this book.

My undergrad economics professor in university years ago said something very important. He said there are only two kinds of people in the world. There are owners and slaves. What did he mean by this? What do you think? [Pause and consider this]

He went on to explain that if you live your life renting, not owning any substantial asset such as a house, a piece of land or anything of material value and then you die, then all your life you were a slave. A slave owns nothing and gains nothing from his or her efforts in life. All of the slave's energies are expended for the benefits of the slave masters. A slave is nothing more than a unit of production in the goal of achieving the ultimate profit. Once that unit of production is no longer capable of producing it becomes expendable.

In plain and simple English this means that any employee or slave, is only as useful as his or her output and the degree to which that employee or slave contributes to the profitability of the owner or slave master.

Thus in many organizations, when an employee can no longer continue doing his or her job, for whatever reason, that employee is immediately replaced. The unfortunate thing is, often, there is no concern for the life of that person and the precious life energy the person expended for the organization. Employers who attempt to justify their callous attitude by claiming that they paid the person for the job, fail to understand how infinitely priceless is the life energy and time of a human being. Nothing on earth can get you more once your time is expired.

Are you a slave? A slave is defined as:

- One bound in servitude as the property of a person or household.
- One who is abjectly subservient to a specified person or influence.
- A machine or component controlled by another machine or component.

I submit to you that if you are living in poverty then you are a slave to CURSE of poverty.

A person who is a slave under the bondage of poverty is bound to servitude in order to just survive. A slave to poverty works hard and gains no personal benefit, much like the parts or components of a machine which work until they run down and are replaced. A slave to poverty is a servant to whoever controls the money whether it is the landlord, the exploitive employer, the abusive spouse, the greedy banker or even the drug pusher.

A very long time ago, I knew a guy who was highly educated with two Masters Degrees and two Bachelors degrees from three different countries, one of which being Canada. He lived in a poor part of the city. His apartment building also housed alcoholics, drug addicts, prostitutes and those in real poverty. Being an immigrant, his accent was strong and he had a very difficult time finding a job.

Have you ever been an immigrant to Canada, the USA, or some other country? Have you or someone you know ever experienced that level of hardship as a new immigrant?

At one point, he worked two jobs just to make ends meet and still it was not sufficient. He worked 6:00 pm to 6:00 am on the weekends plus 9:00 am to 5:00 pm on the weekdays. Monday mornings were the most difficult time for this honest and hardworking man. After he finished working the night shift on Sunday night he would show up for work by 8:30 am on Monday morning even though he was tired or felt unwell.

The earnings from these two jobs were just enough to allow him to pay his rent and pay some money toward his bills and credit debt, and meet his survival needs. For all intents and purposes, he was a slave, and under the CURSE of poverty.

Though he was highly intelligent, he was not money smart, and sadly, Canadian employers did not value his highly educated mind. This along with his inability to find a job paying him a salary commensurate with his high level of education, kept him in poverty. He eventually got ill and could not work. His only income source was his labour, and with that gone, he faced the sad prospect of being virtually homeless. He finally left Canada to return to his native country.

His story is incredibly sad but it does not have to be your story. You've got to recognize the POVERTY CURSE and resolve in your heart to get out of it.

Here is another story. There was a lady who was an immigrant to this country called Canada. She was highly intelligent in the skills of linguistics, and was fluent in several European languages. She also was not able to find work commensurate with her level of education. She worked for years as a receptionist during the day, and not having sufficient money to pay a rent, she saved her money while she slept at friends or wherever she could. She had to work very hard, and still did not achieve much for her efforts. She was also burdened by the fact that her parents needed her financial support, so from the meagre earnings she received, she felt obligated to help them. After years of struggle, she left Canada to work in other fields and eventually came back years later. She had accumulated some savings, but after a few years, found herself right back in the system of poverty, and back under the CURSE.

The lady tried to return to school several times to upgrade her education so that she could work in a different field for more money. Only, each time her efforts were met with unsuccessful interviews, and generally, wasted time and energy. Each time she would return to another low paying desk job with her hopes dashed, and her courage eroded just a little bit further. Each time I heard of her new experience and her dashed dreams, my heart wept for this dear lady.

I also looked at her living environment. Spiritual aliments will manifest themselves in the temporal. Her environment was dirty, crowded, cluttered and her life seemed always cluttered. I remember looking at her place and gasping "Oh my goodness..." and she replied "I allowed you to come here so don't comment about the mess." She was right and I shut my lips together. I wanted to help clean up, and she knew that I'd offered her my help many times before, but she just mentally didn't want to hear anything about her situation.

She became withdrawn and somewhat unfriendly and busy. Eventually we lost touch because she became so busy with struggling to survive in this life, that I felt almost unappreciated for my interest in her well being.

So I ask you again, are you enslaved by the CURSE? If you answered yes, then don't be disheartened. This book is designed to help you come out of the clutches of poverty, from under the CURSE and from the bondage you are currently in.

You will notice that I have written this book from a religious perspective. This is because my relationship with God (Yahweh) has helped me immensely, in knowing the truth, and learning ways which ultimately preserved me, and can preserve you too, if you take this opportunity. The stakes are life and death, and your life is on the line. You've got nothing left to lose but everything to gain. Choose well!

A friend of a friend of mine, worked in the medical profession making a good salary. She worked many hours, but she was poor. She was debt ridden. She took in boarders but each time the situation didn't work out and she was much worse off than before. A family member and I offered to help her many times, but each time she was either too busy or something else came up. Her life is also filled with misery and suffering. Her health was also failing her. How could she get free? It seemed that she was too busy spinning on the hamster treadmill of life to get off and get help.

The CURSE of Poverty can also afflict the rich. The famous baseball player, Curt Schilling earned more than $100 million over his career. He lost it all and is in enormous debt. Mike Tyson, made almost 1/2 billion dollars during his career and then went bankrupt. Can you name others? Michael Jackson, MC Hammer, Easy E, Kim Basinger, and others.

Having enormous wealth placed them in a position where they can hurt others without knowing it, because of their wealth. Like the elephant who is friends with the mouse. The mouse can get accidentally crushed though the elephant never intended it. And without Godly principles to protect them and guard against the forces of evil, the CURSE may come upon the rich. It thus puts an end to the power they wielded with money and avoided further destruction of innocents.

Scripture: Write Proverbs 10:22 (KJV) in the space below.

_____

_____

_____

_____

Here is the hard honest truth, and it is a bitter pill to swallow. You are where you are right now, because it is where you chose to be, and other people who did not care about you, simply aided or enabled you in getting there. But this book is about hope. You are reading it because LOVE has found its way to you.

Hope, Money, and The Law

From my research, I've found that the Mosaic Law, (the Jewish laws today) did not introduce the practise of slavery, but tried to regulate the already existing practise and custom of slavery. This is not an endorsement of slavery. We are all aware that slavery is wicked in today's modern society.

The gospel of Jesus Christ (Yahusha) in the spirit in which it is written, is genuinely hostile to every form of slavery (enslavement). This gospel claims to bring forth the good news of freedom. This freedom is from every kind of slavery known to mankind but there is a twist, it must begin with you. The words of this gospel cannot reach you if you never open your eyes, ears or heart to know it. Thus it can be implanted in you via the eye gate and the ear gate but it must be activated, and this is only by the Spirit of God (Yahweh).

Write the description of Jesus (Yahusha) ministry and purpose as noted in Isaiah 42:6-7 (KJV) in the space below:

_____

_____

_____

_____

_____

_____

The old forms of slavery have managed to be crushed. We no longer have slaves kidnapped from Africa as in times passed. Most countries of the world recognize some form of human rights. Yet, there are new forms of slavery emerging on the landscape, to which those under the CURSE of poverty are susceptible and fall prey. Take this as your warning to be on your guard against all forms of enslavement.

If you have eyes to read these words, hands to hold this book, the means to own this volume, God(Yahweh) has already given you a measure of grace, and wants to work in your life. If you don't have written copies but have an e-book or audio version then be glad also. The message must get to you somehow, because it is the jubilee message.

Poverty's Spiritual Dimension

Poverty has a supernatural dimension as well as a physical dimension to it. Some may be fooled into believing it is witchcraft, obeah, Satanism, voodoo or some other black art which is the source of poverty, but that thinking is faulty. Its supernatural origin is God(Yahweh). He created the law and CURSE of poverty but it has been turned against God's people because they do not understand it. Ignorance of the law will not save anyone from the impact of it.

Poverty is a weapon of mass destruction that has proven itself successful since the days of Pharaoh and Joseph. You read in the Holy Scriptures that the land was under a drought that lasted seven years. Joseph, having received insight from God(Yahweh) that the drought was coming prepared for it under the authority of Pharaoh. When the people were poor and hungry, Joseph eventually purchased all the land, the livestock, and even the people for Pharaoh. He made them all slaves under Pharaoh.

So how do people end up under the CURSE? People end up there through the actions of wicked men, women and powers, and their disobedience to the rules which have been established for their protection from those same wicked powers. But God(Yahweh) is clear. He will not be mocked. He will not allow His people to suffer indefinitely. The sentence is just. This is my warning to oppressors and my hope for the oppressed.

A note about Money

Money can buy you a bed, but not a good night sleep.
Money can buy you a clock but not more time.
Money can buy you a book but not knowledge.
Money can buy you a position but not respect.
Money can buy you medicine but not good health.
Money can buy you friends but not loyalty.
Money can buy you a mate but not love.
Money can buy you blood but not buy you life.

When you have a true perspective on what money is really worth, you see how worthless it is in the course of life.

Course Note: There are 10 indicators of poverty which are covered in lesson 01 of the course. These 10 indicators are applicable across the globe from third world countries to developed countries such as Canada. It is essential that you also recognize these 10 indicators as it is possible that you may fall into a trap. I further distilled these 10 indicators into six(6) indicators for Canada. Write them below:

_____

_____

_____

_____

_____

_____

_____

_____

* * *

Stop And Think

Don't just rush into the next chapter. You may be feeling many emotions right now. Think about them.

Action: Answer these questions. Why do you feel this way? Can you really become free from the CURSE?

Prayer: Dear God(Yahweh), king of heaven and earth, help me to be free from the CURSE.

Affirmation: Today I begin the path out of this wretched CURSE. By the Almighty's help I WILL BE FREE!

* * *

Go to checkpoint #1 and reaffirm your covenant:
www.breakthepovertycurse.com

* * * * *

Are you looking for WISDOM? He that **getteth wisdom** loveth his own soul: he that **keepeth understanding** shall **find good.**
~ Proverbs 19:8

breakthepovertycurse.com

Write Your Personal Insights Here

_____

_____

_____

_____

_____

_____

_____

_____

_____

_____

_____

* * * * *

In our course on Breaking the Poverty Curse at Berkeley Academy, we tackle the topic in more details and give you more fast start money ideas for your cash flow situation. You are simply lacking in some core aspects of fast cash seeding and reaping. Check out the course at http://berkeley.academy/our-courses/

* * * * *

The Necessity of the Curse

Chapter 2

* * *

A moment's insight is sometimes worth a life's experience. ~ Oliver Wendell Holmes, Sr.

Blessed is he that considereth the poor: the Lord will deliver him in time of trouble. ~ Psalm 41:1

There is tremendous sadness in the world because people lack love for their fellow humans. We must love others again as we love ourselves. ~ Vaughn Berkeley, MBA

* * *

Is the Poverty Curse necessary?

Back in the book of Genesis, it says that after the fall of humans to sin, God cursed the earth for our sakes. Why? When the first humans were created, they were given dominion over all the earth to be stewards and care for it. Man's first job was a gardener to care for the garden which God planted and care for all the creatures there. When humans lost dominion over the earth to Satan via the fall, Satan had dominion and man was basically a squatter on his home planet.

The curse of the earth was, it will bring forth thorns and thistles. They hurt and sting but many medicines have been created based on these wild plants so mankind could benefit.

Another curse was that by the sweat of man's effort, the earth will bring forth its produce. Basically, you will reap what you sow. And you need to work to sow the seeds. This again was a benefit to humans because even though it meant hard work, it was a promise that you will obtain benefit from your labour. If it was left up to Satan, mankind would starve in famine. You would work and work and receive no benefit, thus being a slave.

God(Yahuah) is exceptional in the way He brings good out of a bad situation.

So, in answer to the question: is the poverty curse necessary? The answer is yes. It is necessary for several reasons, but it does not need to be permanent.

Now, I'm confusing you, right? I'm saying that it is necessary but it need not be permanent. So that means it is not necessary, right?

No. It means it is cyclical in nature. It is necessary for a season and a purpose, but it is never meant to be a permanent fixture in the life of a person.

It's like the rain. It's good to have rain off and on when you have crops growing in the ground, but you don't want it non-stop for 40 days and 40 nights, right? Just look what happened the last time it rained for 40 days and 40 nights.

Jesus(Yahusha) himself said in the scriptures, "The poor you will have with you always." Obviously, he didn't mean the same poor people living in Israel during his lifetime would be alive today.

Because of the POVERTY CURSE on earth, and just like gravity, it will impact people and work according to its purpose. Thus, you will have the poor with you always as long as there are people who ignore the rules which protect against poverty.

So Why Is Poverty Necessary?

Remember, we're looking at the spirituality of poverty. Consider that a few hundred years ago, literacy rates were low. This meant that a large segment of the population were not able to read or write. If you could imagine yourself in that time in the world, how might things seem to you?

_____

_____

_____

_____

You might see that those people who are able to read and write are able to communicate messages with each other easily. You might also see those people who were illiterate living without access to advanced knowledge and good opportunities in life.

Thus, in order to get ahead, it was imperative that you found a way to learn to read or write through whatever means you could. Parents who saw illiteracy as a problem for their children made sacrifices and sent them to school so that they could learn to read and write. Perhaps if the parents were poor, they sent the children off to be a ward of a rich person in order to learn.

There is a heart-breaking story I learned about in a documentary. Single mothers in a certain country would place their children in the local orphanage because they were not able to provide food for the children during the week. On the weekends, they would bring a little toy or candy to spend time with their beloved child. When a foreign couple asked one of the mothers if she wanted her child to be adopted, she said no. She loved her child but just could not afford to look after the child each day. What she needed was a job to be able to afford to care for her child properly. That mother and many others like her, were using the orphanage as a boarding house for their children because they were so poor. The foreign couple created jobs for those mothers.

Poverty exists today and has existed from ancient times in order to help mould the character of all those in the presence of poverty. Even those who were not poor were expected to learn a character lesson by being in contact with a poor person.

Poverty is meant to cause those afflicted by it to reflect on their life and their purpose. It is meant to cause the person to turn from their bad ways and choose the path of goodness.

Here's Raymond

Here's a story told to me by Raymond Aaron. He said that he had a very promising start as a young man. After graduating from university, he authored a math textbook that was mandatory for first year students. After teaching he was a highly paid consultant. He also dabbled in real estate. And by the age of 40, he was broke and living at home with his parents.

He says he was so broke that he went to the park to sit during the summer because he didn't have to pay to sit on the park bench. He was poor and broke. Did he give up? He felt like it.

Fast forward to him now. He's the Canadian author of two Chicken Soup for the Soul books, he is the author of a book in the "for Dummies" franchise. He is also a successful real estate investor with over 1000 real estate transactions.

Without the POVERTY CURSE causing him to pause and reflect on his life, he might have gone in a totally different direction. Who knows what direction his life might have taken.

Now Raymond Aaron charges enormous fees to teach people how to make money and holds all day workshops where other people come in to sell the audience ways to make more money. Raymond is 72 years now with a hot young wife and he is not financially poor any more.

I mention Raymond here because I know that there may be some of my readers who are in their mid-thirties, or approaching 40 or older who have not yet achieved a life of worth. If you are under the POVERTY CURSE, then use that experience to sit and reflect on your life, please. I'm glad you're reading this book now because I am praying for you that God(Yahuah) would touch your heart and mind to reveal the lesson He wants you to learn.

It Enables You To Reset Your Spiritual Compass

For you personally, if you are afflicted by the POVERTY CURSE, it will enable you to doubt the things you were doing. It helps to cut out the noise which filled your life. It gives you a moment to think about what's real and what's true. It can give you the chance to reset your spiritual compass to the right direction.

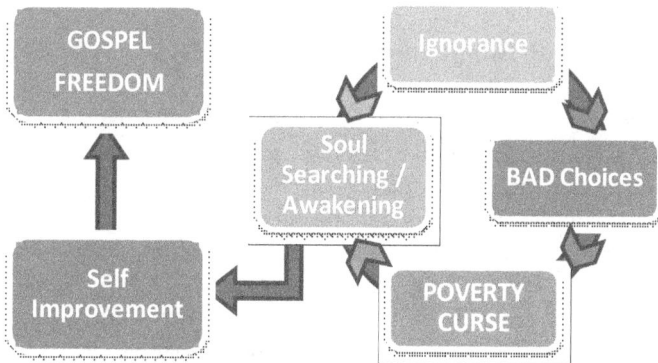

Look at the chart. We discuss this in great detail in the course. You can see that it is a cycle beginning at Ignorance and going around and around. If you get to the soul searching/ awakening but you never take that opportunity, then you remain in ignorance and under the CURSE.

Those who don't find that awakening, remain in ignorance and make more bad choices which lead to the poverty CURSE.

Those who choose the path of Soul searching and awakening, move on to self improvement, and eventually to the Gospel Freedom promised to those on the divine path. Don't confuse prosperity with godliness. There are some who have sold their soul for earthly wealth and are still under the Poverty Curse.

Once you experience the awakening, and you move to self-improvement, then you can move to the GOSPEL Freedom which is freedom from the CURSE.

Write what the bible says in John 8:32 below.

_____

_____

_____

A Runaway Entertainer

Ever hear of the very talented comedian Dave Chappelle? He gave up a $50 million contract and fled to Africa to live in poverty for a short time. Why? You can Google his talk and watch his interview on YouTube. Basically, he refused to sell his integrity for $50 million. He chose temporary poverty by buying a plane ticket and running away to Africa. People thought he went crazy. The mainstream media were presenting all sorts of speculations about what happened to him. Was it drugs? Was it a mental breakdown?

He needed to reset his spiritual compass. He needed to realign his current life with his inner integrity and purpose. He made a choice to go broke to Africa.

I know that for those of you living under the POVERTY CURSE, and it is not your choice, it seems like a terrible thing for you. Believe me, poverty is not something to be indulged permanently. So if you are still in poverty, then you need to hit the pause and reset button.

It Enables Those Blessed With Abundance To Develop True Compassion

Poverty allows people who have abundance to have an opportunity to share with others who have nothing. It is God(Yahuah) giving people a chance to open up their hearts in love to others. Every day, rich and successful people come into contact with people who are living under the curse and in need. Yet, some of those rich people have grown so callous that their hearts are made of stone. They lack any compassion for those who have less than they.

Those people ultimately will face the hell spoken of in the Bible because they are allowing money to become their god and they worship it. The only way for them to reverse this hardening of their heart is to give to the less fortunate.

Consider this Bible teaches about a rich young man who sought answers in Matthew 19: 21-22. Write it in the space below.

_____

_____

_____

_____

_____

_____

True compassion could start small with $5 or a hot lunch on a cold day. Maybe you can give someone your umbrella if you see them standing in the rain while you are driving in your comfortable car. This actually happened to me a while back. I was driving one autumn morning and it was pouring rain. I saw two teens standing by the road waiting for their bus, getting soaked. I pulled up and called the guy over and told him they could use my umbrella to shelter from the rain until the bus comes. I told him just throw it in the grass when he leaves and I'll collect it later when I drive back that way.

Later on that day, I found my umbrella neatly folded next to the house. Did I feel good to help those kids out? Yes. Were they blessed? Yes. Did I receive a blessing from God for my kind heart? I'm sure I did. So you're probably thinking, what would I do if they kept my umbrella? I would get a new one in the dollar store. It was a cheap umbrella that I could afford to lose if they kept it. I've loaned my umbrella to friends stuck before and had it gone until the next year, so I am thankful for the cheap dollar store umbrella.

The more wealth God(Yahuah) has allowed a person to acquire, the greater the responsibility on them to administer compassion and show love to others. God(Yahuah) will ask them to give account one day. Miserly people who have an evil eye will perish with the rest of the evil-doers.

Don't believe it? Jesus(Yahusha) told the parable of the Good Samaritan. People named it "The Good Samaritan" but the more appropriate name for that parable is "Knowledge of Scriptures Without Love and Actionable Compassion is Evil" but that title is too long and not as catchy, I guess.

Look at the lesson Jesus (Yahusha), messiah, taught that day.

The ordinary guy who got attacked by robbers could be any of us. We all go through periods of attack by the enemy that leaves us feeling heartbroken or battered and bruised. The priest/pastor came by first. He had an abundance of blessings. He had knowledge of scriptures, respect and honour in the community, nice garments, and a feeling of being at peace.

And what did he do? He ignored the wounded person, crossed the road to the other side and went on his way. The one who was supposed to be so blessed was also so devoid of compassion and love.

The same thing happened with another person, the elder/deacon. Again, no love or compassion.

The Samaritan guy knew about God (Yahweh) and had worshipped from a distance. Yet God had seen his heart and blessed him with some materials (financial means). When he saw the wounded man, his heart was filled with love and actionable compassion.

The Samaritan went to help the man. He bandaged his wounds. He put him in his wagon to take him to safety. He put him in a safe place to recover. He paid his bill so that his needs would be attended to.

What a striking demonstration of love!

The man had fallen due to the CURSE, but the Samaritan brought relief and hope for a better outcome. Without the CURSE, we might not have had the opportunity to see the true heart of each individual in the story.

The poor is universally despised, even by their own family sometimes.

Thus, when you have money, you have lots of friends willing to help you spend it but when you are poor, those friends vanish. Poverty reveals their true heart and intention. It also tells you a lot about yourself.

* * *

- Acts of God
- Taxation
- War and Crime
- Inflation
- No Access To Monetary Tools
- Government Corruption
- Rich Exploitation of the Poor
- History of Poverty
- Government Mismanagement
- No Education / Skills
- Overpopulation
- Laziness
- Substance Abuse
- Sickness / Disease
- Pride / Arrogance

| Macro Level | Industry | Community | Micro Level |

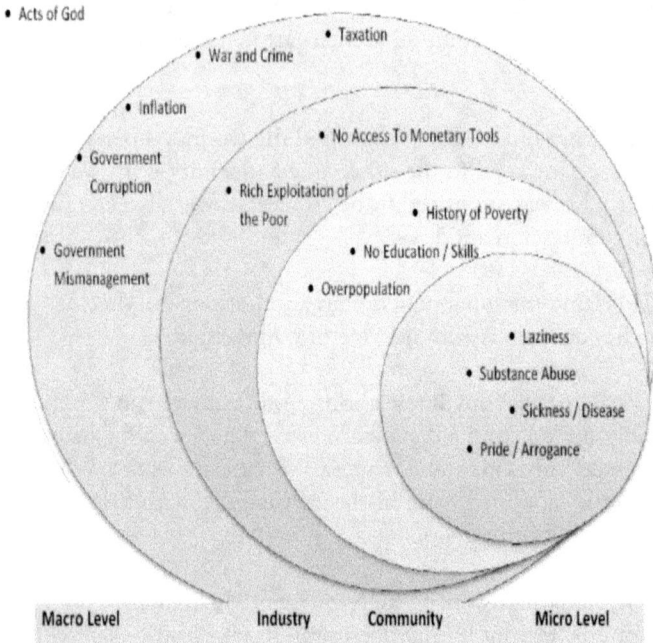

Figure 2-1: Factors That Impact The Poor   Source: Author

Factors That Impact The Poor
Course Note: The chart showing the Factors that Impact
The Poor was taken from my research on poverty and
microfinance. I wanted to look at some of the reasons why
the poor remain poor over generations. I've broken them
down into categories. You have the micro level, the
community level, the industry level, and the larger macro
level. And outside of that you have Acts of God. In the
course, I cover the way these factors work. List the five(5)
categories below.

_____

_____

_____

_____

_____

_____

_____

It is interesting to note that these factors can affect anyone regardless of skin colour, race, ethnicity, or gender. Note the majority of the factors are man-influenced. This means that human beings also have the capacity to fix the poverty CURSE problem if their hearts, minds, and spirits were in the right place. Where you do you see yourself on this spectrum?

* * *

Stop And Think

Don't just rush into the next chapter. This is your time to pause and reflect.

Action: Answer these questions. Have you ever neglected to help a poor person? Can you really become free from the CURSE by giving to the poor?

Prayer: Dear God, king of heaven and earth, open my eyes to the needs of the poor around me and help me to be free from the CURSE.

Affirmation: Today I look for a person to help and begin the path out of this wretched CURSE. With the Almighty's help I WILL BE FREE!

* * *

Go to checkpoint #2:
www.breakthepovertycurse.com

Write Your Personal Insights Here

_____

_____

_____

_____

_____

_____

_____

_____

_____

_____

_____

* * * * *

In our course on Breaking the Poverty Curse at Berkeley Academy, we tackle the topic in more details and give you more fast start money ideas for your cash flow situation. You are simply lacking in some core aspects of fast cash seeding and reaping. Check out the course at http://berkeley.academy/our-courses/

* * * * *

Assessing The Poverty Curse
Chapter 3

* * *

O generation of vipers, how can ye, being evil, speak good
things? for out of the abundance of the heart the mouth
speaketh. A good man out of the good treasure of the heart
bringeth forth good things: and an evil man out of the evil
treasure bringeth forth evil things. - Matthew 12:34-35

More people talk themselves into failure than talk themselves
into success. - Zig Ziglar

If I could learn to do the right things correctly, I would only
wish that I had learnt those things as early as possible in my
life. Failing that, I'd start learning them right away. ~ Vaughn
Berkeley, MBA

* * *

This chapter is entitled Assessing The Poverty Curse because
like a person who is ill needs a doctor, so a person under the
CURSE of poverty needs a healer. However before you can
see the healer, you need to know what are the symptoms you
are exhibiting, pretty much the same way the medical doctor
needs to know the symptoms you are experiencing, in order
to diagnose the disease and prescribe a treatment.

To tell the doctor you feel bad without any further
information will not help the doctor diagnose you. To say,
I'm poor will not help you much either. This is because you
neither know nor understand what is keeping you under the
CURSE of poverty. So let's begin to take this journey to
identify some of the possible symptoms.

Remember in the previous chapter we touched briefly on the
categories of the factors which influence poverty. Well, the
micro level, is your level. It is where you MUST begin your
journey.

What are some of the personal causes of the CURSE of poverty?

LAZINESS: This is defined as inactivity resulting from the dislike of work. It is also defined as apathy and inactivity in the practise of virtue. The gospel teaches that the lazy person will have the CURSE of poverty come upon him.

Proverbs 6:10-11   Proverbs 10:4
Proverbs 12:24   Romans 12:11

Note the key points of each verse below:

_____

_____

_____

_____

_____

_____

_____

_____

_____

Now be honest with yourself. If you were doing a self test for breast cancer or some other ailment, you'd be honest with yourself. You wouldn't say oh that lump is nothing. Now, you're doing a spiritual self-test and you've got to be honest with yourself, if you want to get out from under the CURSE. If you're not putting in the effort when you know you should, and you're not physically sick, then you've probably developed a laziness habit.

Do you know of people who find all kinds of excuses why they cannot work? You say, try this job, and they say, I can't because that won't work. Perhaps you say this person is hiring, and they say that they refuse to work for minimum wage. There was a guy I know of who was poor. Yet, when he was told about work, he refused to do the work because he felt the pay for too low for him. Yet, he lived off the charity of others begging them for a financial support to help him pay his bills or buy food. He was young and strong but suffers from laziness.

WICKEDNESS: This is defined as being morally bad in principle or practise, having committed unrighteous acts, or being extremely bad or unpleasant in degree or quality, and being morally bad or wrong. Simply put, it is doing bad willingly and without remorse or regard to the consequences of your actions on others. The gospel teaches that the CURSE of poverty among others, will come upon the wicked.

Psalms 12:8   Proverbs 12:3   Proverbs 12:6
Proverbs 12:7   Romans 12:14   Romans 12:19

Note the key points of each verse below:

_____

_____

_____

_____

_____

_____

_____

You will notice that in describing wickedness I've put in positive and negative verses. This is because the negative verses illustrates explicitly the way of the wicked, while the positive verses causes the mind to discover the way of the wicked, by looking at the opposite meaning.

This is your self test again. Perhaps in doing this self test you will realize that you were wicked in the past, but now you want to change. I encourage you and applaud you for taking this step. Recognizing error and choosing to correct it in oneself is at the very heart of the journey to unite with our divine God (Yahuah).

FAILURE TO ACCEPT CORRECTION: If you fail to accept correction, then you basically say that you wish to remain in your current state of affairs. No one is born knowing the perfect way. So to end up at the destination where you are now, takes some effort or lack thereof on your part. If our mistakes have led here, then it is in our best interest to take heed of good advice, and to make the needed correction. Like a ship with its rudder stuck, thus causing the ship to go off course, we too went off course. Now the rudder can be fixed if we are willing to accept correction from the great navigator and heavenly GPS (Gospel Positioning Saviour).

Proverbs 13:18   Proverbs 3:11-12   Proverbs 12:1
Proverbs 15:10   Revelation 3:19

Note the key points of each verse below:

_____

_____

_____

_____

_____

_____

_____

_____

_____

Examine yourself again. Do you feel insulted whenever someone tries to give you good advice? Do you feel insulted now reading this book? It is a spirit of rebellion and pride that is at the root of this feeling. Be honest with yourself now, it is your moment of truth.

GREED: Greed is defined as an excessive desire to acquire or possess more than you need or deserve. It is a reprehensible acquisitiveness or insatiable desire for personal gain. Simply put, if you want more and more, you will eventually fall prey to the CURSE of poverty or worse.

Proverbs 1:19   Jude 1:11   1 Timothy 6:9-10
Ecclesiastes 5:13-14   Luke 12:15-21

Note the key points of each verse below:

_____

_____

_____

_____

_____

_____

_____

_____

Greed is really such a seductive emotion. It is like a drug. It stimulates the brain when that one extra item is gained. There is a law that describes the level of satisfaction one gets when one consumes one more of an object. This law dictates that the more one consumes, the less satisfaction is gained by each additional item.

For example if you have 100 bananas and were starving; when you ate the first one you would feel extremely satisfied. When you ate the second banana you'd feel almost the same level of satisfaction. By the time you ate the 50th banana you would not be feeling that satisfied. And by the time you got to the 100th banana you may very well feel disgusted by it and may not even want it.

This law works in a rational person but someone with greed is never satisfied so at the 50th banana, the person would still not be satisfied and would want just one more. At the 100 banana they would still not be satisfied even though they might be feeling sick. Under greed, you would not feel disgusted by the 100th banana as a normal person would, but instead feel a burning need for one more hoping that one more will make it better.

Like a toilet tank with a broken shut-off float, the greedy person never gets to the shut off point. But there is yet hope for you, if you are in this greed condition, and the CURSE is upon you.

Richard Pryor's Interview: I saw an interview with Richard Pryor on YouTube and the interviewer asked Richard about Racism. Richard's answer was distilled so simply that a child could understand it. Richard basically said that greedy people magnify the differences between people like skin colour in order to keep people from talking about the real problem: those greedy powerful people.

This is tremendously insightful. Greed is a cancer of the soul. God(Yahuah) desires that His people do not succumb to it.

DISOBEDIENCE: Disobedience is the refusal or failure to obey. Disobedience is comparable to rebellion. Why would this be important? It is because those who desire your good, may give you good advice, but you refuse to follow it, because it will mean changes to your life. Reading this book may contain items that make you aware of areas where you need to change, but you may not want to. This will mean that you will further delay your deliverance from the CURSE.

Here are some of the many CURSES enumerated in Deuteronomy 28.

- CURSED in the city AND CURSED in the country
- Your tools CURSED
- Children CURSED, Crops CURSED, Livestock CURSED
- CURSED when you go in and when you go out
- All the works of your hands CURSED
- Plagued with the CURSE of wasting diseases, fevers, inflammations, boils, tumours, festering sores, madness, blindness, confusion of mind
- CURSES of Blight, Mildew, Heat and Drought
- CURSED and defeated by your enemies
- CURSED and unsuccessful in everything you do
- CURSED in relationships; you will be married to one woman and another will ravish her
- CURSED in your house, you will build it and not live in it
- CURSED to face cruel oppression all your days
- CURSED with enslavement
- CURSED with hunger, thirst and dire POVERTY
- CURSED with cannibalism of your own children
- CURSED by fearful plagues, harsh and prolonged disasters, lingering sickness
- CURSED with no rest or peace and full of dread night and day

Disobedience to Yahuah's laws then, is a huge gateway, through which a flood of CURSES may enter. But you may say that this is a lot of hooey, after all, no parents literally eat their children today. Well, I'm afraid that parents are still eating their children today, but it is not physical eating.

When parents drain the money of their children because the parents are so much CURSED, then this is "eating your children." That is, eating their financial future.

When a couple is married for many years, and the marriage ends with one spouse leaving to live with another person who has financial means to provide, then this is the CURSE.

When you lie awake at night unable to sleep because you may lose your house or creditors have started calling you for money then you are under the CURSE.

When the wicked system of taxation and usury is placed on you, and interest is added to interest in an attempt to enslave you and cruelly oppress you, then you are under the CURSE.

But here's hope! Romans 10:21 states, 'But about Israel God says, "All day long I stood ready to accept people who disobey and are stubborn."' Turn from disobedience and give obedience a try. If you're under the CURSE then do it now for your own life and the lives of those you love.

SELFISHNESS: This is defined as a form of stinginess resulting from a concern for your own welfare AND a disregard for the welfare of others. The combination of both is key. It is at this point that you demonstrate that you have become destructive to yourself and to those around. You are in real danger of coming under the CURSE.

Proverbs 28:27   Deuteronomy 15: 9
Isaiah 5:8-10   Deuteronomy 24: 14-15

In Proverbs 28:27 the Bible teaches that one who "gives to the poor will lack nothing, but he who closes his eyes to them receives many CURSES" Deuteronomy 15 also speaks to forsaking the need of your brother, because you are concerned that you will not get a return or repayment.

Deuteronomy 24 tells us that we should pay the labourer at the end of each day he/she works, because he/she is poor and needs his/her money. It warms that if this person cries to God (Yahuah/Yahweh) against you, it will be counted as sin against you.

This knowledge if properly understood can cause thousands of employees to open a doorway to a CURSE against their employer. A quick note here for employers. The practise of withholding someone's salary for a month, a fortnight, a week, a few days or even a few hours longer than the day in which it is earned, is unbiblical and I submit to you, it is the reason why so many ordinary people are getting deeper into the CURSE.

Ever wonder why people go to Pay-day loan companies? It is because they have no money and choose to borrow until the pay day! Why should they borrow money from another while the employers withholds what is rightfully theirs? This practise is basically theft and is wrong. Think about it in this scenario. Suppose an employee works for a company and they withhold two weeks salary which is $500. The employee is poor and needs that money to buy food, clothes, or pay rent so they can't wait the 14 days to get it. The employee then goes to the pay-day moneylender to borrow the $500 and pays a $50 fee to the company. So the poor person has spent $550 while waiting for their $500 paycheque. When they get paid the $500, they go to the pay-day moneylender to pay off the debt. Then they are broke again plus $50 behind. And the next pay cycle the scenario happens again and so on. This is wicked and stealing from the poor.

It is a practise that is meant only to benefit the employer, while robbing the employee of his/her duly earned reward. Also note that your withholding their income and deductions is comparable to theft of your employee's property. Though modern society and culture has normalized and sanitized this wicked practice, the standard of heaven is as true now as it was from the beginning.

The money is all the employees' and the Bible is clear on that point. It is therefore highly disturbing that you, employers, are putting yourself at risk of falling under the CURSE.

In Isaiah 5, God tells of the complete and utter selfishness of the rich and their impending destruction. He says, "Woe unto them that join house to house, [that] lay field to field, till [there be] no place, that they may be placed alone in the midst of the earth! In mine ears [said] the LORD of hosts, Of a truth many houses shall be desolate, [even] great and fair, without inhabitant."

Here God (Yahweh) is foretelling that the real estate developers who build house to house and lay field to field in order to make obscene profits, will face desolation. Does this manifestation of the CURSE seem similar to the meltdown of the US real estate market? God is not mocked.

All real estate developers over the world who build tiny expensive places for people to live, so they can squeeze more profit out of a piece of land, had better take heed.

There is another wickedness I have seen among selfish real estate agents. In Ontario, the newspapers ran a story about the scandal. Selfish and greedy real estate agents are artificially hiking up the house prices in order to extract more money from the poor novice buyers. There's even been calls for fines, and harsh penalties for agents who abuse buyers this way. The selfish real estate agent is not thinking about the harm they are doing to a poor family by saddling them with extra debt just so they can squeeze a higher commission fee from the deal. God is not pleased by these things and the agent could fall under the POVERTY Curse.

LICENTIOUSNESS: This is living a life in excess and in disregard for rules, standards and moral standards. You probably saw someone at least once in your lifetime who has lived life without regard for anything. This person spends without a care for tomorrow, drinks alcohol until completely drunk, or womanizes until completely broke. If you are behaving like this then you need to check yourself, because you will surely be under the CURSE of poverty.

Proverbs 29:3   Luke 15:13-14

- Proverbs 29:3 states, "Whoever loves wisdom makes his father rejoice, But a companion of harlots wastes his wealth."
- Luke 15:13-14 states, "And not many days after, the younger son gathered all together, journeyed to a far country, and there wasted his possessions with prodigal living. But when he had spent all, there arose a severe famine in that land, and he began to be in want."

It is a good time to note that an exhibition of one or more of the previously mentioned symptoms in any combination could be the reason why you are under the CURSE.

Ellen White (Adventist Home, 1952) states that,

Near the close of this earth's history, Satan will work with all his powers in the same manner and with the same temptations, wherewith he tempted ancient Israel just before their entering the Land of Promise... Satan is determined to destroy with his temptations--to pollute their souls with licentiousness... he sets his hellish powers and his agencies at work and overthrows them upon the weak points in their character, knowing that he who offends on one point is guilty of all, thus obtaining complete mastery over the entire man. Mind, soul, body, and conscience are involved in the ruin. If he be a messenger of righteousness, and has had great light, or if the Lord has used him as His special worker in the cause of truth, then how great is the triumph of Satan! How he exults! How God is dishonoured!

If you are guilty of one, you become guilty of all. Beloved, BEWARE because you are surely headed for that direction, without proper treatment. The CURSE if not upon you yet has been dispatched by the unchangeable laws of the universe.

Only the mercy of God (Yahuah) holds back the deliverance of the full impact of the CURSE. Know that the devil (Lucifer/Satan) did not create the CURSE. He opportunistically exploits it for his purpose.

God set the CURSE in place to withhold the wicked, but if you are counted among them, you will suffer their fate.

Christ (Yahusha/Messiah) now stands between you and the tidal wave, pleading with you to turn from your ways and to Him, to be safe from the CURSE. That is the reason you are reading this book now! Wake up!

* * *

Health is one of the areas that can be impacted by the Poverty Curse. Are you doing the things to protect yourself or to expose yourself to the CURSE? Paul's book is one book that can help you understand the

What Does The Bible Say About Health?

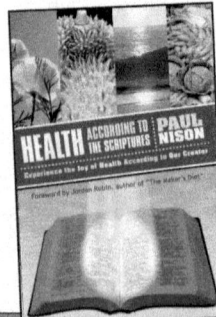

Find out In Paul's book!

Available at online bookstores

concept of health according to the scriptures!

My Life Strategy: Part 1

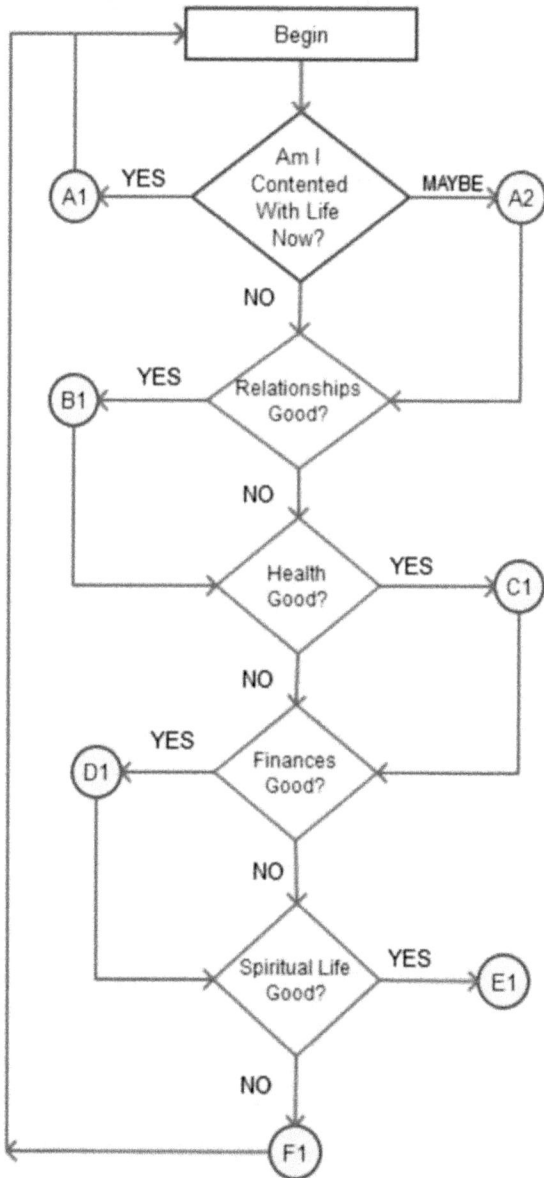

Course Note: The chart showing the My Life Strategy - Part 1, is meant to help you reassess your life and focus on an annual basis. In the course, we discuss the deeper meaning of each of the Coded Areas, A1 through to F1.

In the space below, write your answer to each of the questions. Then use the space to write why you answered yes or no.

_____

_____

_____

_____

_____

_____

_____

_____

_____

_____

_____

_____

_____

_____

* * *

Stop And Think

Have you seen areas of your life that are increasing your risk of exposure to the CURSE? Maybe you're already in too deep, and feel there is nothing to be done. Don't believe that lie. You're reading this book right now because LOVE wants you to be FREE.

Action: Today, take a hard look at your life, and list the things in it that could be keeping you under the CURSE. Fight them one by one until you slay them.

Prayer: Almighty God(Yahuah), please help me overcome the things in my life that are keeping me under the CURSE. Help me become FREE. Save me from the CURSE for your name sake. Amen.

Affirmation: Today I have taken the first step to eliminating the CURSE-attracting attributes in my life and by the Almighty's help, I WILL be FREE.

* * *

Go to checkpoint #3:
www.breakthepovertycurse.com

Write Your Personal Insights Here

_____

_____

_____

_____

_____

_____

_____

_____

_____

_____

_____

* * * * *

In our course on Breaking the Poverty Curse at Berkeley Academy, we tackle the topic in more details and give you more fast start money ideas for your cash flow situation. You are simply lacking in some core aspects of fast cash seeding and reaping. Check out the course at http://berkeley.academy/our-courses/

* * * * *

Vaughn Berkeley, MBA

The Mental Dimension

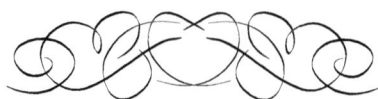

II

Are you living under POVERTY BONDAGE?

How long wilt thou sleep, O sluggard? when wilt thou **arise out of thy sleep**? Yet a little sleep, a little slumber, a little folding of the hands to sleep: So **shall thy poverty come** as one that travelleth, and **thy want as an armed man.**

~ Proverbs 6:9-11

breakthepovertycurse.com

The Congregation (Body of Believers)

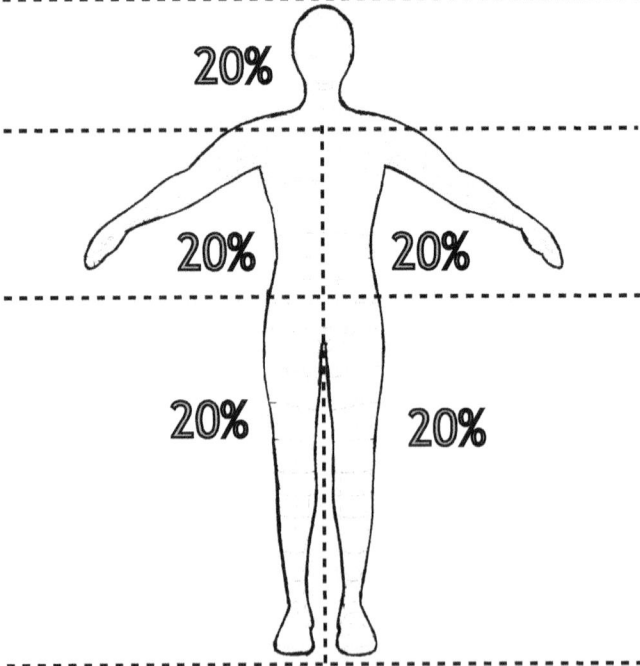

20%

20%   20%

20%   20%

Desolation & Despair
Chapter 4

* * *

And it came to pass, when the time was come that he should be received up, he steadfastly set his face to go to Jerusalem, And sent messengers before his face: and they went, and entered into a village of the Samaritans, to make ready for him. And they did not receive him, because his face was as though he would go to Jerusalem. And when his disciples James and John saw this, they said, Lord, wilt thou that we command fire to come down from heaven, and consume them, even as Elias did? But he turned, and rebuked them, and said, Ye know not what manner of spirit ye are of. For the Son of man is not come to destroy men's lives, but to save them. And they went to another village. ~Luke 9:51-56

Kindness in words creates confidence. Kindness in thinking creates profoundness. Kindness in giving creates love. ~ Lao Tzu

My heart weeps daily for all the pain and suffering that poverty causes in the lives of men, women, and children. Surely God(Yahuah) sees from heaven. ~ Vaughn Berkeley, MBA

* * *

This chapter is called desolation and despair because I want you to see the final result of the matter. When you know the end, and your current point, you can plot a line to show you your current course. If you see your current course is leading you to the place you don't want to go, then you can take action to change your course.

The average Christian and non-Christian is under attack by a systematic onslaught of techniques which lead to being under the POVERTY Curse.

I want you to imagine something for a moment. In your mind, visualize a huge field as far as the eye can see and you are standing in the middle of it.

This field is bone dry. There is nothing growing on it. The earth is parched and cracking all around. As you stand in the middle of this field and you look, you slowly turn. You observe every direction. It all looks the same. It is all dry earth as though the land had been experiencing a drought for many years.

Now in your hand, you have a sack of seeds. These are good seeds and you can use them to grow a huge crop. The problem is you can't grow them because the earth is dry and you have no water supply. With each passing moment, you feel hunger growing in you. Now you are feeling a choice setting in, do you try to plant the good seeds to bring a harvest or do you eat the seeds to satisfy your hunger. This visual is the CURSE of Poverty!

That is exactly what happens to those under the CURSE of Poverty. You are in a huge field with a sack of seeds but you have to eat them to live because the field will not yield its fruits to you. And it is like that when you are trapped in poverty.

You have a little bit of money that you saved from your job and you want to invest it or do something to make it grow BUT you have to eat today or starve. So you use part of it to buy food or pay rent or pay an important bill.

In 2010, Dr Evans Morgan, gave a financial seminar which opened my eyes tremendously. Dr Morgan was the auditor for the church and he visited various churches. He visited the black churches, the Chinese churches, the Filipino churches, and so on. At each church when he gave a lecture on finances, he would take an informal survey of members by show of hands.

Here's some of the amazing data he shared with us.

Among Christian church families, approximately 40% of them were overspending every month. Do you get that? Four out of 10 Christian families were spending more money than they make every month. This meant that as time progressed, 4 out of 10 Christian families were heading to the destination of financial desolation. This speaks volumes to us as a family of believers when we allow 4 out of 10 of our brethren to walk down the path to financial ruin without trying to help lighten their load and bring them back onto sure footing. It says there is no Christ-like(Yahusha-like) love there but selfishness. Heaven forbid.

Dr Morgan mentioned that 20% of Christian church families he had spoken to were on the verge of divorce due to the money problems. Those families were having a few issues but the money problems just made the problems worst till the couple argued all the time. Frustration and a loss of hope and a fullness of despair often leads people to take out their frustrations on the ones closest to their heart. And hurtful words, once release can do so much damage that it is difficult to repair.

Dr Morgan also noted that 50% of Christian church families had marriages that ended with divorce. It seemed like the church was no better than the rest of the world where it is about 50% of marriages end in divorce.

He also noted that 90% of the church families that divorced sited financial difficulties as one of the reasons for the divorce. Get that? Nine out of 10 divorced Christian church families were saying that financial reasons were one of the significant factors that led to their divorce.

He noted that 40% of Christian church families were paying more than $2800 a year in interest on debt (excluding mortgages). That's 4 out of 10 church families who are giving away $2800 every year to pay interest on credit card debt. That money could be used to make life a little easier. It could be used to help foster church missionary work. It could be used to start building an inheritance for your children and children's children. Our people are perishing while they are enriching wicked and evil persons.

He also mentioned that 37% of Christian church families were in debt. Again, that is about 4 out of every 10 church families are in debt. The debtor is servant to the lender according to scripture. How can a family serve God(Yahuah) with love and joy when they are being forced to serve others to fulfil the obligations of the debt? God(Yahuah) have mercy.

And this other statistic he mentioned was that 19% of Christian church families had no savings. Did you get that? No savings. Zero. This means that 2 out of 10 church families are just one significant catastrophic incident away from desolation. Think about that. A car accident, being injured on the job, a chronic illness, a mortgage payment doubling, or any kind of catastrophe could place that church family on the verge of bankruptcy. God(Yahuah) have mercy.

Do you recognize the implications of these things on you personally? Does your church elders, deacons, or pastor recognize the implications of this on the entire body of believers?

If we think of the church families as the body of Christ. We can call the congregation The Body of Believers. Church families are the cells which make up the body, much like a human body. The body can be divided into five equal parts.

The head and neck would represent 20%, the left arm and left ribs represent 20%, the right arm and right ribs represent another 20%, the left leg and left waist represent 20%, the right leg and right waist represent the final 20%.

Now we know that in a healthy and fully functioning body, we can run, sprint, jump, climb, and move toward any goal.

The body of Believers is supposed to move forward to the goal of spreading the gospel and winning souls for the kingdom of God(Yahuah). If we say that 40%, 4 out of 10 church families were overspending every month, that means that 40% of the body of Christ was bleeding out every month. Look at your arms and legs on your body. If your two legs were cut and bleeding, you would stop the bleeding wouldn't you? Could you run at your best with both legs bleeding? Of course not. So why as a church family in the body of Believers, do we allow 40% to bleed money every month. Look at the human body drawing at the start of this chapter to help you visualize this.

Let's look at the 20%, 2 out of 10 church families with no savings. That's like having one of your arms broken. The wrong move or sudden unexpected impact would be devastating to the injured limb. Not to mention it would cause tremendous pain and suffering. That's the situation those 2 out of 10 church families find themselves in. Wouldn't you make every effort to protect your own arm if it was broken? You would try to prevent it from any impact and would carefully move it. Then why are elders, deacons, pastors, church members, committee leaders, and others in the body of believers failing in looking after the broken limb of church families with no savings?

I don't believe that it is simply because people don't care about others. I think it is that all of us, including deacons, elders, and pastors feel like we are in the middle of that barren field and there is nothing we can do.

I'm here to say that by the grace of God(Yahuah) it is not so. It is possible to reverse this situation. Because even if an arm is broken, the other limb can help dress it and protect it. The brain can still coordinate the needed biological functions needed to heal it.

If we as a church family fail to help members of the body of Christ falling under the CURSE of poverty, then you will see them leave the church because the church is fruitless.

Here's a story to illustrate this point.

Long ago, I knew of a woman who was a very dedicated believer in her youth. She was raised in a semi-Christian home and had a long history with the church. However, her life took some bad turns. She quarrelled with her semi-Christian parents, got kicked out when she was legally old enough to be on her own, lived from place to place on the kindness of strangers and friends, and due to multiple health conditions, was not able to secure a way out of poverty. She was living under the CURSE of Poverty.

Somewhere along that journey, she gave up on God. She came to believe that God does not exist because she found no compassion or support in her life. All of her early attempts at being a good Christian feels as though it was wasted.

And because she grew up in a semi-Christian family and suffered so much, it is harder to try to win her back to God (Yahweh). The sum of her past experiences have driven her away from God. There are numerous times when the church family should have intervened with compassion to help her. She should have learnt of the principles of the Poverty CURSE.

She believed her life is filled with misery and hopelessness with only brief moments of joy to keep her from ending her own life. For her, it is a victory just to be willing to face another day.

This is very real problem that the church as a body will have to address. The church will lose sincere believers when the financial pressures of the world spring up and choke the life out of their faith.

Mind you, she did demonstrate qualities that keep her under the Poverty Curse. She broke so many of the universal rules concerning prosperity that the CURSE came by her own doing.

What about you?

Even non-Christians can become so overwhelmed with financial pressure that they begin to suffer from depression. They can feel bouts of hopelessness.

The POVERTY Curse does not discriminate between black or white, or Canadian or non-Canadian, or adult or child, or male or female. It can attack anyone who is ignorant of the universal principles which govern it.

Are you presently standing in your own desolate field? Do you feel like you are trapped because the little seeds you have can't possible be of any help to you?

With all my heart, I want you to know that there is hope for you. It starts with a true friend or partner. And it includes education.

If you have signed your covenant at the beginning of this book, you've enlisted my help as your spiritual guide. My prayer is with you for your freedom from the CURSE.

The second component is getting an education. I'm not talking about a $100,000 university education that leaves you with a mountain of student debt. I'm talk about a much more affordable course I have designed to help you master the principles and skills you need to come out of the POVERTY CURSE.

Reading this book is your foundation in your education. Then taking the course is building on your foundational education. It is an investment in you. I have a specific time when we allow enrolment so you want to get on the waiting list. You can read more about it after the final chapter of this book.

* * *

D _____

E _____

P _____

R _____

E _____

S _____

S _____

Course Note: The acronym above is significant when we look at meaning of desolation, depression and despair in the context of the POVERTY CURSE.

In the space above, write the meaning of each letter in the acronym. Use the space below to write how you can use it in your day-to-day life.

_____

_____

_____

_____

_____

_____

* * *

Stop And Think

Don't just rush into the next chapter. Examine your emotions. Why do you feel this way? Can you really become free from the CURSE?

Realization: Now I understand truly how much bigger than myself this problem is. I recognize that I am part of a body in Believers and need to call upon brethren for help. I must also be willing to help other believers. I have taken the steps in this chapter to move forward out of the curse.

Prayer: Almighty God(Yahuah), I now understand the severity of the CURSE. Please forgive me for my sins and wilful disobedience of your laws. Teach me of you and your ways. Help me to follow you wholeheartedly. Renew my heart, my mind, my body and soul for you. Break this CURSE for your name sake. Thank you for loving me enough to intervene in my life at this present time. Please fill my life with your love and help me share all you teach me with others around me. Blessed be Yahuah, God Almighty. Amen.

Affirmation: Today I know the truth and I will ask the body to help or help another in need. I AM FREE.

* * *

Go to checkpoint #4:
www.breakthepovertycurse.com

* * * * *

Write Your Personal Insights Here

_____

_____

_____

_____

_____

_____

_____

_____

_____

_____

_____

_____

* * * * *

In our course on Breaking the Poverty Curse at Berkeley Academy, we tackle the topic in more details and give you more fast start money ideas for your cash flow situation. You are simply lacking in some core aspects of fast cash seeding and reaping. Check out the course at http://berkeley.academy/our-courses/

* * * * *

Children should be guided into healthy eating for their mind and bodies at an early age. This delightful story helps parents expose their children to

healthy eating concepts as they follow the adventures of two best friends. Get this book online.

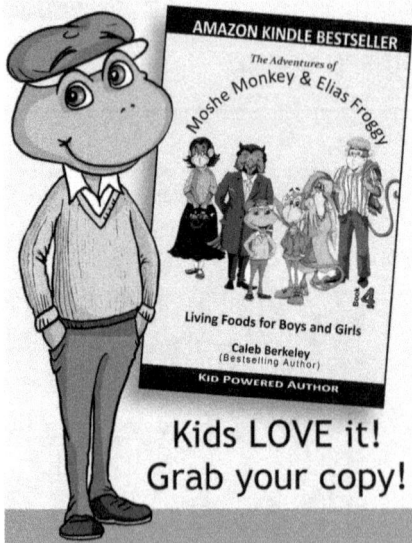

Broken Relationships

Chapter 5

* * *

The sacrifices of God (Yahuah) are a broken (humble) spirit: a broken and contrite heart, O God (Yahweh) thou wilt not despise. ~Psalm 51:17

No person is free who is not master of himself. ~ Epictetus

God (Yahuah) seeks the heart. Love dwells there. If love is absent, then God(Yahuah) is absent, and evil manifests there. ~ Vaughn Berkeley, MBA

* * *

This chapter is about relationships. But you're probably asking what does relationships have to do with the mental dimension of the POVERTY Curse. The mental aspect of our being is very much significant in our actions. All actions begin as a thought which is then made manifest. Therefore we ought to study relationships with our mental dimension of the POVERTY Curse because it's easiest to measure and get feedback.

Relationship To God(Yahuah)

This relationship while it is essential to every human being, must be taught to a child and practised as an adult. How is your relationship to God (Yahuah) lately? Do you have a relationship with the creator of heaven and earth?

The relationship to God (Yahuah,Yahweh) is one that is as old as the creation of humans. The scripture teaches that God (Yahuah) created humans in his own image and crowned them with a clothing of glory in the garden of Eden. The first man, Adam, was given dominion of the entire world and appointed a steward of the world. Scripture teaches that God(Yahuah) presented him with the animals and whatever Adam named them, that is what they were to be called. What an awesome mind to be able to name all the animals and remember an elephant from a tiger. Man was also given the task of tending to the perfect garden God himself had created.

When the first man recognized that all the animals had a mate but he was unique, God(Yahuah) provided him with a female companion that would be his mate for all his days on the planet. Together, the man and the woman were both blessed to be fruitful and multiply on the face of the earth. Thus humans are endowed with the power to reproduce themselves.

The scripture teaches that the angels in heaven do not have this capability. Jesus(Yahusha) answered a question. It was based on a scenario about a woman having been married to seven brothers as each had died without any children. They wanted to know whose wife will she be in eternity. Jesus(Yahusha) answered that they shall be like the angels neither married nor given in marriage.

Matthew 22:29-30   Mark 12:25

The first human was clothed in the Glory of God(Yahuah) like a celestial being. When sin entered the world, humans lost that clothing of glory that was their initial clothing. Scripture tells us Adam and Eve hid from God(Yahuah) when they heard his voice in the garden because they were naked. They were without their clothing of Glory.

Our relationship to God(Yahuah) clothes us in spiritual ways we do not yet perceive. And as God (Yahweh) is a Holy God, He requires that we do not defile ourselves in order to dwell with him in holiness.

Sin has separated us from God(Yahuah) and broken our relationship. The divide was beyond our capability to repair because it was the domain of earth separated from the kingdom of heaven. Suppose the Queen of England has a dispute with the Prime Minister of Canada, can an ordinary person like you or I repair that breach? No. They must work out the dispute using the protocols established for such an event. Likewise, when Satan became ruler of Earth usurping Adam's rightful birthright, only Jesus(Yahusha) could repair the damage by his atoning sacrifice.

God (Yahuah) has been waiting with open arms for all his lost children to return to Him. God (Yahweh) is a king. Heaven is a kingdom not some cloud place where people dance on clouds in togas playing harps. We as children of the most high God must act in accordance with the protocol expected of us. Being called sons and daughters by the adoption offered through Christ (Messiah), we have the broken relationship being healed.

The duty and responsibility falls on us to learn how to live in the kingdom of heaven, to study its precepts and principles so that we would be good heirs to the kingdom and ambassadors of heaven on earth while we are still here.

Many of the traditions and things people do in their lives are rooted in ungodly practices. These rituals are against the kingdom of God(Yahuah) while lifting up the kingdom of the exiles of heaven(Satan and his angels).

For example, every adult knows Santa Clause is fake, yet this fakery turns millions of Christian adults around the world into LIARS who lie to their children by telling those trusting and innocent children that this fake deity brings toys for the children on December 24th every year. When you celebrate or indulge in this lie, you deny the true living God, Yahweh(Yahuah) and break your relationship with him. December 25th is the ancient pagan day of Sun worship not the birthday of Jesus(Yahusha) so participating in that falsehood is against the kingdom of God(Yahuah).

Some Christians also celebrate Halloween. Heaven forbid. Even if you allow your child to dress up as a princess or superhero instead of a devil, you are still participating in the festive activities of the holiday. Any occultist will tell you that Halloween is their high witchcraft/worship day. It is their day for worship to the exiles (Satan and fallen angels) of the Kingdom of Heaven. Any Christian who participates in that event by handing out candy or dressing up in a costume is acknowledging the exiles of heaven (fallen angels) as deities while denying the true God (Yahuah) as the only sovereign and ruler of heaven and earth. This is breaking their relationship with God (Yahuah).

The true relationship to God, Yahweh(Yahuah) is the prerequisite for all other good relationships on earth. Without it, other relationships end up lacking the divine influence of holy love.

In the Bible, we learn of two brothers who both had spoken to God(Yahuah). Those brothers were Cain and Abel. Both knew God(Yahuah). Both knew his requirements. Then came the test. Both were required to bring a sacrifice at a determined time on the same day. Abel brought his sacrifice, an unblemished lamb and offered it on the altar of sacrifice while his brother Cain brought fruits and veggies and offered it on the alter of sacrifice. Abel's sacrifice was accepted while Cain's was not. Cain was angry at this and God(Yahuah) spoke to him explaining why his offering was not acceptable. Later on we learn that wicked Cain killed his righteous brother Abel. God(Yahuah) pronounced a CURSE on Cain for this vile act.

What's the big deal about how to worship anyway? Didn't both brothers talk to and hear the voice of God(Yahuah)?

Yes, both brothers did talk with God(Yahuah) but the difference is one listened, obeyed, and had understanding. That was Abel. Cain on the other hand did not have understanding even though he had heard God(Yahuah) speaking to him. The sacrifice was meant to represent the coming of Jesus (Yahusha) to take away the sin of the world. Thus an unblemished lamb was required for that sacrifice not an offering of fruits and vegetables. The symbolism is lost when you change the symbols which is what Cain did. Cain's disobedience to God(Yahuah) led to his jealousy and hatred of his brother and ultimately it manifested in the murder of his innocent and righteous brother Abel.

In Hebrews 11:4 we read, "By faith Abel offered unto God a more excellent sacrifice than Cain, by which he obtained witness that he was righteous, God testifying of his gifts: and by it he being dead yet speaketh."

Many professed Christians in the world are following the path of Cain in the manner in which they worship God(Yahuah). They are following pagan and ungodly rituals and traditions which are not what God, Yahweh(Yahuah) wants his children to partake of. These ungodly things have been mingled with the church worship. Thus these Christians claim to worship God, Yahweh(Yahuah) but their worship is polluted and filled with sin and iniquity. Therefore even their prayer is an abomination to God(Yahuah) in heaven. They are hurting their relationship to their loving God(Yahuah), our creator. What is necessary is a call to repent and turn back to God(Yahuah) in humble obedience like Abel.

Genesis 4:1-15   Hebrews 11:4   1 John 3:12
Jeremiah 3:6-7   Jeremiah 10:1-4   Jude 1:11
Jeremiah 10:20-22

Summarize the key message of the bible verses in your own words in the space provided:

_____

_____

_____

_____

Relationship To Parents

This is the second most important relationship we experience in our lifetime. It is one given to us at birth but one that began nine months prior to our birth. For many of us, while we were still in the womb, we were loved by our parents.

The scripture teaches that children are a blessing from God (Yahuah). The fruit of the womb (children) is his reward. Parents are given a blessing from God (Yahweh) when they have a pregnancy that will produce wonderful fruit if cared for properly.

Yet, many parents globally, reject God's gift by committing murder of the child in the womb. They use a pretty and sanitized word in order to hide the gruesome act of murder. It's called abortion. The scripture teaches that according to God's instructions, anyone who kills a child in the womb is guilty of murder and his blood is required for the act. The unborn child is not the mother's right or choice, the unborn child is God's gift and God (Yahweh) despises killing a child in the womb.

Because people have allowed such an abominable disrespect of the sanctity of life in the womb, it has impacted the way people view parents or parenthood. If an unborn child's life is worthless, then by association the perception is that the parent of that child is worthless.

Any parent that supports the murder of babies in the womb gives their own children the message that the parents are of little value. This subtly undermines the relationship.

But wait, there's more!

Parents are the first role models of children. Children model and mirror the behaviours they observe in the home. They learn to eat, poop, play, communicate, and worship in the home.

How important is it to model the right behaviours for your children? Scripture tells us that. "The Lord, the Lord God, merciful and gracious, long-suffering, and abundant in goodness and truth, keeping mercy for thousands, forgiving iniquity and transgression and sin, and that will by no means clear the guilty; visiting the iniquity of the fathers upon the children, and upon the children's children, unto the third and to the fourth generation."

Why does God (Yahweh) mention the third and fourth generation? Because the habits parents form in their children within the home can last as long as 3 or 4 generations. That is how powerful the home life is and why the relationship to parents is second under the relationship to God (Yahuah).

If a parent is an alcoholic or heavy drinker, their children may have a higher propensity to adopt drinking as they get older. If a parent is abusive, the children may have a propensity toward that behaviour.

What about parents that are wicked and spiteful? Can you have a good relationship with them? You have to have the love of God(Yahweh) in your heart but still exercise caution so that their destructive tendency does not hurt you.

As a parent how can you have a godly relationship with your children?

Firstly, you have to transform yourself by the renewing of your mind daily in the study of the Holy Scriptures. You've got to do your spiritual best in order to model it for your children. Is that possible? Yes.

Think of this. When a parent has two children and the last child is allergic to milk or nuts, doesn't the parent turn the entire house into a dairy free or nut free zone in order to protect the child with the allergy? Yes, loving parents do that. The danger is real and the motivation is there.

If you are not treating the spiritual condition of your home with the same kind of urgency and importance as a deathly allergy, then the fault lies with you. So do step 1.

Step 1: Renew your own mind with daily study of the scriptures.

Next, you need to pray for your children daily and also teach them to pray for you and each other. Prayer is a powerful tool in the defence of the home as well as a tool to attack the enemy of good. A family that prays together stays together. So do step 2.

Step 2: Pray together and pray often

Teach children how to be useful part of the running of the home. Every child can and should be given age appropriate chores which build confidence and character. A four year old can use a hand-broom and dustpan to sweep up some dust or the four-year-old can be given a damp cloth to wipe the table after eating a meal. A 7-year-old can wash dishes after meals. An 11-year-old can make a salad for the family dinner. A 15-year-old can clean the car or mow the lawn.

There are no shortages of responsibilities in the home where children can receive practical training for life. And children love it when their parents congratulate them on the job well done. This fosters love, appreciation, and an appreciation for work. So do step 3.

Step 3: Help children be useful in the home

The final step in healing a relationship between parents and children is to exercise love. If you were a terrible and selfish parent and your children are adults now, then show them you can be loving by offering to do whatever you can for the grandchildren. Offer to babysit them, offer the chip in and pay for soccer or dance lessons. This will show your children that you have matured past your selfish behaviours.

Step 4: Show love in abundance.

When parents fail to follow the right guidelines in their
relationship nurturing with their children, it fractures the
relationship leading to a fractured community, and a divided
nation. Scripture teaches us that a house divided against itself
cannot stand. The CURSE thrives in this splintered
relationship.

Relationship To Spouse

The spousal relationship comes after the parental
relationship as God (Yahuah) has declared this. In the
garden of Eden, when He presented Eve to Adam,
God(Yahuah) pronounced, "for this reason, a man should
leave his father and mother, and be joined to his wife."

Now I know what some naysayers would be thinking. How
can parentship take priority to marriage since God (Yahweh)
joined Adam and Eve in marriage in the garden before they
were parents? It's in the words of God's proclamation.
God(Yahweh) is a king. His Words are proclamations
because of his authority. By his word, he defined and created
parenthood before even completing the marriage ceremony.
It is found in the phrase, "for this reason a man should leave
his father and mother (parents)." Thus God(Yahuah)
prioritized the parental unit even before Adam and Eve were
parents and parenthood is an eternal institution to be
vigorously defended just as marriage is vigorously defended.

When you leave the umbrella of your parents, it is to create
your own life with your spouse. This relationship is
established by God (Yahweh) and is given a high
importance. From this spousal relationship, parenthood is
derived, children are nurtured, and communities are
strengthened.

Each of us are called to be disciples of
Christ(Yahusha/Messiah) in our daily living. When the union

of two individuals take place to form a new family unit, then the love of Christ(Messiah) can be modelled for others to see.

Remember earlier on in the book, I mentioned that financial pressures were responsible for many Christian marriages ending in divorce. Don't you think that it is essential that before you select a life-long mate, you have a guide to assess what traits must be in your mate.

When you ignore the fundamental principles of selecting a mate, then you create a way for the POVERTY CURSE to affect you. Poverty in the marriage relationship is not only about money but about the spiritual and emotional needs of the marriage.

Firstly, the Holy Scripture, does not recommend people in the body of believers be married to persons in other religions. The different belief systems and approach to worship will create a conflict as time goes on. I have had older friends who ended up with a broken marriage after numerous years because they were of different faiths and could not agree. They stayed together until the kids were grown up then divorced. The marriage was loveless and lifeless, under the CURSE of Poverty.

Story time: An older lady spoke to me one time about her marriage. She was a Christian married to a man who was not a Christian. Their marriage ended after 20+ years with him running off with a younger woman who appealed to him. The woman told me he was not a Christian. Here it is easy to see that without the shared love of God in both the man and the woman, the marriage is doomed to fail whether it takes one year or 20+ years.

I know of women who married men who did not have a heart for God(Yahweh). These men subsequently beat them and abused them. Yet, they remain with the ungodly man for whatever reason. One time, a woman I knew had an abusive husband. She would call me when she hit a rough patch. I would give her advice when I did not know about the physical abuse. When she finally told me one day that her husband was choking her when they were fighting, I told her to separate from the man for her safety and her kid's safety. She disregarded my advice and went back to him. I was heartbroken and worried about her.

Sadly, I told her do not contact me anymore about her problem because it caused me pain and heartache to see it every time and knowing she won't follow my advice. She refused my Godly advice to her even though I had been her spiritual advisor and friend more than a decade. She still calls me from time to time because I have only ever showed her love and compassion. But she knows not to complain to me about her ungodly marriage. When we talk it's like old best friends talking and we can laugh and update each other on our lives but she is forbidden to seek my advice on her marriage because she refuses to accept my godly advice.

Choosing the wrong person to join yourself to can lead to a life of misery, without love, joy, and without the blessings God (Yahuah) intended for you to receive in the marriage relationship. The marriage devolves into a carnal and sexual organism where sex is used as a means to keep it together. But when the husband or wife gets too old, or too unattractive, or too inconvenient, they face a high risk of being discarded like garbage. God(Yahuah) does not want his children to be in this kind of marriage union.

There are godly principles for selecting the right kind of mate. I compiled this guide in my 20's under the inspiration of God and deep study of my bible. I read this guide every week to keep it fresh in my mind. It helps men select the right mate and women be wise.

Thus Step 1: Select The Right Mate

Once you select the right mate that God (Yahweh) would approve of, what is next for you? You have to nurture the marriage relationship properly. Do you know that the bible suggests that married couples take a one-year honeymoon? In Deuteronomy 24:5 it states, "When a man hath taken a new wife, he shall not go out to war, neither shall he be charged with any business: but he shall be free at home one year, and shall cheer up his wife which he hath taken."

If only God's people would follow that method today. How much of a blessing of love and joy would marriages receive. The husband and wife should take a year off their responsibilities in order to love and comfort each other in their new life.

Today people get married and take a one or two week honeymoon and then go back into the grind of daily life. This is undermining the marriage and inviting opportunity for the POVERTY CURSE later on in life.

Thus the second guide for building a strong relationship is take a very long honeymoon. If you cannot take a year, then try 9 months or 6 months. Make that an essential part of forming a strong marriage at the beginning of a marriage. Use that time to get to know each other in love and exercise godly principles together.

Thus Step 2: Take A One-Year Honeymoon

The next important principle is to respect your spouse in accordance with the position God(Yahweh) has granted to them in the household. Women have authority over the home and a man must help but not interfere. Man has power and authority regarding spiritual matters and the woman must help but not interfere.

To interfere is to undermine the roles that God(Yahuah) desires each member of the union to model for their children. To respect one another, there must be trust, patience, and love.

If a woman thinks her man is wrong, he is not to be berated or belittled in front of the children, the family, or the public. And the same is true for the husband. He should not shame or flame his wife in front of their children, friends, family, or the public.

When there is friction in the marriage relationship, it bleeds over into all aspects of your life. A man will perform worst on his job. A woman will perform poorly at her job. Children will become troubled. Other relationships will be fractured. Leaving home will feel like a joy and returning home will feel like a torture. This is not what God(Yahuah) intended married life to be. When the marriage relationship exists in the CURSE, the fruit is always a bad outcome. And no amount of sex can heal that terrible spiritual union of man and woman under the CURSE.

Thus Step 3: Respect Each Other's Position In The Home

Remember relationships are about mutual respect and love. And this is paramount between a husband and wife. The two flesh become one. If you disregard this you open the door for the broken relationship and the POVERTY Curse in your life.

Relationship To Children

Children are precious to God(Yahuah) even before they are born. Did you know that God taught in the Bible that a pregnant woman should not drink alcohol? In Judges 13, verse 7, the angel of God tells Samson's mother, "Behold, thou shalt conceive, and bear a son; and now drink no wine nor strong drink, neither eat any unclean thing: for the child shall be a Nazarite to God from the womb to the day of his death."

In the womb, the child is to be protected. The diet of the mother must be clean because the child will be impacted.

And what about after being born. The Bible tells us in Psalm 22:9, "But thou art he that took me out of the womb: thou didst make me hope when I was upon my mother's breasts." God(Yahweh) loves children and is watching over them and gives them hope. Children are an inheritance from God (Yahweh). Again in Psalm 127:3, we read: Lo, children are an heritage of the LORD: and the fruit of the womb is his reward.

No woman has gotten pregnant accidentally, EVER in the history of the world. No child growing in the womb is an accident of God(Yahuah). Adults may consider it accidental but God does not.

In today's modern society many people are childless or suffer miscarriages. This is very sad. When God (Yahweh) has blessed you with children, you must thank him and acknowledge your gratitude for such a blessing.

Remember, Jesus(Yahusha) even stood up for the children when his disciples were preventing the little children from coming close to him. Jesus(Yahusha) is the Christian example of life on earth. He was born as a baby and grew up as a child and then went into adulthood.

Can we learn anything about childhood from Jesus' example? Yes. As a youth, he worked with his step-dad, Joseph in the carpentry business. He learned the trade and the skill of his family. As a youth, he was also engaged in a careful study of the holy scriptures.

In order to build a good relationship with your children, it is the duty of the parent to ensure that the Holy Scripture is a daily study for the child, just as going to secular school in the day is important for academic study.

By the time, your child is 12 years old, he or she should be as grounded in the scriptures as Jesus(Yahusha) was when he stayed in the temple have deep discussions with the rabbis.

Vaughn Berkeley, MBA

When a parent with the proper relationship with the children, does the right thing. Many, if not all, of the childhood baggage that adults bring with them into adulthood would be eliminated. Today, we have "force-ripe" men and women who inhabit adult bodies but have so much issues from their childhood, it is like they never grew up. The apostle Paul in 1 Cor 14:20 writes,"Brethren be not children in understanding howbeit in malice be ye children, but in understanding men."

Just to be clear on the meaning of that verse by Paul. Little children forgive and forget in a snap. If they are angry with you now, in 10 minutes they will hug you and tell you they love you. It's all water under the bridge with them. That is for children that are raised correctly in sound doctrine and principles. As they get older that same attitude of forgiveness and peace will continue on.

As parents of sound understanding you must ensure that your children have access to the spiritual nutrition of the Word of God daily.

According to the work of Maria Montessori, children have an absorbent mind from age 0 to 5 years. By that I mean from the womb before birth till age 5. Their minds are sponges absorbing all the stimuli of their environment. They can learn 5 languages fluently without an accent during that time if taught following the correct method. They can also absorb the power of the scriptures during this time as well. It is your parental duty to teach your children well to make our society better.

Thus Guide 1: Ensure you study the Holy scriptures with your children daily.

Do not use the work of God as an opportunity to neglect the relationship with your children. Pastors, elders, deacons, ministry leaders, and workers, all have a solemn responsibility to nurture a godly relationship with their children and not neglect them. When any church worker

101

spends too much away from their children doing ministry work, then they are proving themselves unfit for the kingdom of God.

Even if you are not a church worker but find yourself spending more hours at work than you do with your children, you are destroying the relationship with your children. Do you know any workaholic husbands or wives? Are you one? **Stop it.**

Thus Guide 2: Give your children the time needed to help in their growth and development.

Have you ever seen children undisciplined in matters relating to food? Some children eat non-stop even though they are overweight or obese. Some children are hooked on candies and sweets. Some children refuse to each fruits and veggies.

When I was growing up in Catholic school, some of my classmates were Muslim. During their holy festival they would fast daily. I would always be intrigued by my fasting classmates because I had never had the reason or opportunity to fast. We're talking about youth aged 11 to 15. So it is possible for parents to teach their children to be discipline in matters relating to food. If my classmates who were of a different faith were learning to strengthen their mind against the temptation of food, you should teach your children this same discipline.

Doesn't the parent of a child with a nut or dairy allergy teach that child to not take anything from school friends with dairy or nuts in them? When parents teach their children to exercise self-control in what they eat, they are teaching them a principle for success in spiritual matters and physical matters.

The scripture encourages us to eat for strength and not for gluttony. We are also directed to separate the clean from the unclean so that we might eat only what is beneficial for our health and well-being.

I have heard children of this generation being described as the first generation that have a lower life expectancy than their parents. What a tragedy! When this is being said about our generation of children, then it is a failure of parents to stand up against this trend. Children are now suffering from old folk diseases. When I was a little child growing up, you never heard about children with heart disease, obesity, diabetes, arthritis or other similar diseases. If you did hear of it, this was an exception to the rule. However it seems like today the majority of our children are sick and the passage of time is only making them sicker.

Food is a huge component of that. Some children are digging their graves with their forks because of the unhealthy diet they consume daily.

If your child grows up with a weakness toward food or sicknesses from eating poorly, then the child may blame you and resent you for not showing them the right way during their youth and making things so much more difficult for them in their adult years.

Thus Guide 3: Help your children obtain mastery over their food.

When a parent fails to show their children the basic principles of life, their relationship with the child is not to the fullest. Have you heard of some parents who lavish their child with everything the child could want only to see that child become a spoiled and selfish adult? Relationship begins with consistency and instruction in righteousness.

Relationship To Extended Family

Have you ever heard the saying "In-laws are outlaws"? I was told this by a semi-Christian fellow many years ago. Funny thing about this semi-Christian man is that he used his parent-in-laws to babysit his child for over a year. He ate free meals from his in-laws whenever he could. It is quite hypocritical and selfish to use your in-laws for your convenience while saying in-laws are outlaws.

That is not to say that there are no boundaries. Your extended family such as in-laws, siblings, aunts, uncles, and others are all important to building the sense of community. However, their influence should never be so strong that it leads you or your family to stray away from God (Yahweh).

Extended family can impose a tremendous amount of peer pressure on individuals in order to get them to conform to the strongly held beliefs of the family.

Consider this. When a family member converts to veganism, the rest of the meat eating family always mocks and ridicules the person's choice. Family gatherings are the hardest because all the person's favourite meat meals may be prepared in an attempt to tempt the new vegan to eat meat or eggs or cheese.

When you have family and they have different religious beliefs, they may feel inclined to have you part-take of their religious traditions. This can create conflict especially if they have no desire to learn about your firmly held beliefs in God (Yahuah) and his ways.

So with extended family, you have to show love and exercise wisdom.

If a family member is in need of help and it is within your power to help without compromising your firmly held beliefs then go ahead and help them. Love, is a healing balm for family relationships.

Relationship To Friends

The relationship to friends is a bit like the relationship to extended family. However, you can choose your friends but you can't choose your family.

If you can choose your friends, then shouldn't you exercise some godly wisdom in the selection of friends that will help you to live a more meaningful life? Birds of a feather flock together don't they? And the scripture teaches us that iron sharpens iron.

If you want to grow more than your current state whether in business, or spiritually, or in any area of your life, you need to surround yourself with friends who are knowledgeable in that realm. If all your friends have no ambition in life, and don't see any problem with that outlook on life, then if you want to be better, it will be an uphill struggle for you while living in that environment.

The Bible teaches friendship with Christ(Yahusha) is enmity with the world. This is because the ways of the true believer are vastly different from the ways of the unbeliever or semi-believer. The world represented by the Spiritual leaders of the time as well as the secular leaders represented by Rome, all played a part in the death of Jesus(Yahusha). Jesus said, if they hated him, they will also hate the followers of Jesus(Yahusha).

Can a believer and a non-believer be friends? What kind of friendship can they have together? When one friend feels a burden to talk about their God and the other friend feels a burden to ridicule their friend's God. It is a very difficult situation to find oneself in. It's like meat eaters and ethical vegans being friends. It is very tough because being around the cooked carcass of animals is highly unnerving to the ethical vegan.

There are stages of friendships and indulgences.

If you find that you are honest with yourself and you are a person easily persuaded by those around, then you must be ultra-selective in your choice of friendships. Your friends will have the power to lead you thus you need to ensure that you only have friends that will lead you in the right path.

At this level, you can be comparable to a youth in spiritual development. You are growing spiritually but need to be guided correctly before you go down the incorrect path. Find and hold on to godly men and women during this phase. It is important to your development of character and your spiritual development. You must be firmly ground in the spiritual truths of God (Yahweh) so that his holy light will shine in you and you will be as a light onto the world. You are a receiver more than a giver at this stage so it is imperative that you receive sound doctrine and good precepts. Your friendships during this stage have to nurture you.

During this stage you do not want to be embroiled in darkness so that it stifles your light. Do not be friends with thieves, liars, adulterers, drunkards, evil people, angry people, greedy people, or those who would entice you to do wrong. This is for your own spiritual safety because you are not strong enough to stand for the kingdom of heaven at this stage. You risk losing your own soul if you hang around them as they entice you to follow them.

It is like flying in a plane with a child next to you. If the plane begins to lose cabin pressure and the oxygen masks fall down from the ceiling. What do they tell you? Even though your urge might be to place the oxygen mask on the child first, that is the wrong response. You could risk losing consciousness and dying. The correct response is to put on your own oxygen mask then place the oxygen mask on the child. Thus you will save both your lives.

With the list of bad friends mentioned above, you may want to tell them about the love of God(Yahuah) in your life and his saving power. But the situation is like the air is coming out of the cabin and you won't be effective to save them if you don't first study to show yourself approved of heaven. Once you are passed the youth stage of spiritual development, you are more grounded in your beliefs. Your light from heaven is burning brightly within you. It is not at its fullest but it is bright enough to draw others to you. You

are able to stand for the truth when asked about it. You are not able to defend your point against a master of darkness but you are able to stand your own with ordinary people who are looking for answers in a world of darkness.
At this stage, you have two kinds of friendships. You have friendships where it is about nurturing those who are weakest. Compassion for the lost, the downtrodden, the marginalized, the poor, are a part of those friendships in your life. You also have friendships where you are still being mentored and growing in deeper spiritual mysteries of heavenly things.

You are still growing spiritually but you should have begun producing fruit. Your fruit is the friendships that leads others to the love of God (Yahuah). You may only produce a few fruit but that is a sign of the spiritual truth growing in you.

The final stage of spiritual development as it relates to friendships will enable you to have achieve mastery of your craft. You are fully grounded in the truths, protocols, and principles of the kingdom of heaven and Almighty God (Yahuah). You are fit to accomplish the great commission of Yahusha(Jesus) to go out into the world and make disciples.

Like the 72 disciples that Jesus(Yahusha) sent out two by two, you will return to him with great joy saying, "even the devils flee from us in your name." At this point, there is mastery in the physical realm and the spiritual realm. Your friendships here produce a bountiful fruit for heaven. You are doing the work of the disciple of Yahusha(Jesus) of helping the poor and needy, speaking up for the oppressed, helping captives become free, and spreading joy. Friendships at this level are based on respect, gratitude, love, loyalty, and hope in the saving power of the kingdom of God(Yahuah).

When you fail to attend to relationships the correct way, then you increase the risk of the POVERTY CURSE. Consider the example of a group of vagabond Jews in the book of Acts. It states in Act 19:13-16, "Then certain of the vagabond Jews, exorcists, took upon them to call over them which had evil spirits, the name of the Lord And the name of Jesus, saying, we adjure you by Jesus whom Paul preacheth. And there were seven sons of one Sceva, a Jew, [and] chief of the priests, which did so. And the evil spirit answered and said, Jesus I know, and Paul I know; but who are ye? And the man in whom the evil spirit was leaped on them, and overcame them, and prevailed against them, so that they fled out of that house naked and wounded."

This is an example of a POVERTY CURSE moment. They were defeated by a high wicked power because they only dabbled in friendship with Christ and did not know Messiah as their friend and saviour. They were wholly ignorant of the power and authority of the kingdom of Heaven thus the exiles of heaven (fallen angels/evil spirits) got the upper hand on those gentlemen. How many Christians today are living in the same powerless manner? Ponder it.

Follow the pattern for building lasting friendships that allow you to shine your light so others may see the way before them. Failure to do so will cause broken relationships and leave way for the POVERTY Curse.

Relationship To Work

God(Yahweh) appointed work for the empowerment and enhancement of human beings. It was a blessing to humans. Good work is meant to strengthen the mind, body, and spirit. Is it then not obvious that the relationships we engage in at the workplace have an impact on the holistic development of the human being?

As with the process we outlined when selecting friends, a similar thoughtful process must be applied in selecting a working environment. Money is never to be the paramount factor in whether a job is to be taken or rejected. However, it is not a factor to be completely ignored either.

Too many people have jumped for a job because they thought the money was great but it ended in their distress and created a manifestation of the POVERTY CURSE.

When work is not aligned with what God (Yahweh) has in mind for you, the work itself brings on stresses from every angle. There is no peace at the workplace, no peace when you leave the workplace, and no peace when you force yourself to return the next day. If all you do is go in to earn a paycheque to pay your bills, then you are a slave under the POVERTY CURSE.

Consider this example of when the workplace is aligned with God's will for a person. The patriarch, Joseph, was in prison when he was called out to interpret Pharaoh's dream. The dream was about the 7 fat cows and 7 skinny cows which ate the 7 fat cows. God (Yahuah) was working in this situation. Pharaoh was so impressed with Joseph and the fact that God was with him that Pharaoh appointed Joseph second in command in the entire kingdom. No one except Pharaoh was higher in authority than Joseph. The relationship Joseph had in the workplace with his boss Pharaoh was a good one and Joseph had the trust and confidence of his boss. Joseph did not have to deny his faith in God (Yahuah) in order to do the job well. In fact, it was precisely because Joseph had a close relationship with God (or a link-up as youth would say) that Joseph got the job.

The true believer in a strong relationship with God(Yahuah) will bring supernatural blessings and prosperity to the work environment in addition to their natural skills and abilities. Any good boss or entrepreneur or business owner should jump at the opportunity to have a true believer on the payroll. Every dollar invested in that person will be returned many times over.

On the flip side, as an employee, you have to be extra careful about who you work for. You do not want to use your God given blessings to enrich the evil person or oppress the innocent. You have a duty and a responsibility to judge the leadership of the workplace as well as the fruit of the organization. If evil fruits are manifested from the company or entity, run away from that place as you will not be blameless in the day of judgement.

Do you find yourself among co-workers who do not appreciate you? Is your boss always unhappy with your work or finds a problem even when the work is fine? Do you find yourself having to stifle your religious convictions because it is not tolerated in the workplace? Then this work environment is not the place for you to be, period.

The POVERTY CURSE will try to force you to select any kind of job in order to try to ease some of your worries but the job you select will give you more stress, damage relationships with friends and family members, and may be making you sick with each passing day.

Even if you are working in what seems like the perfect job but are not growing spiritually and have no opportunity for the light of God(Yahuah) to shine in you, then you are like a candle placed under bed. You are hindered from your true calling.

One final thing for you. Should you quit a job if it forces you to compromise your deeply held spiritual beliefs? Absolutely yes. To compromise your deeply held spiritual beliefs is to give up a piece of yourself. And if you do this enough times, there will be not enough left of you. Trust in God(Yahuah) to bring you to a better job where your dignity, and deeply held spiritual beliefs will remain intact.

Thankfully as you go through this book, you will learn of the truths you need to address the POVERTY CURSE in your life.

Relationship To Business Investments

As we come off the topic of work, I want to touch on the subject of business investments or business partnerships. As

God(Yahuah) begins to bless you with financial means, there will be people who come to you with business opportunities which require you to invest your money, your time, your skills, or your connections.

Be very careful in this area. Some of these people may be genuine God-fearing people who are brothers and sisters in the body of Believers. But others may be workers of the kingdom of the exiles (Satan).

We are instructed not to partner with wicked men and women in order to enrich them and further their wicked desires. Wicked people will lie and deceive, or entice the simple God-fearing person to join with them in a venture.

Imagine this with me a moment. Suppose you were blessed with some financial means, and a person came to you to ask you to invest in a movie production. You would be one of numerous investors, and there are hundreds of people on the cast and crew. The person tells you the movie will make millions and you will be repaid many times over what you invested. It's a sure thing. However, the movie contains promiscuity, drunkenness, lying, stealing, adultery, murder, fornication, blasphemy, and other immorality.

Should you invest in such a movie? Here's how to analyze this. God(Yahuah) will hold every person involved with the creation of that movie accountable for their part on the day of judgement. The actors saying the lines and committing the sin on screen will be judged. The crew providing the equipment will be judged. The screen writers, directors, producers, will all be judged. And yes, the investors who supplied the money will be judged too. As many people are caused to sin by the creation, promotion, and distribution of that movie, so will the punishment of that sin be magnified.

Thus, as a believer, you are prohibited from investments in such ventures. In fact, in proverbs 1:10-16, the scripture teaches that if sinners entice you, do not consent. What is this enticement? The allure of easy money or quick money. It goes on to say if they tell you let's wait for innocent blood and consume them and fill our houses with spoil (loot or ill-gotten gain), don't do it. They say join with us and we shall have one purse. Think about 2000 years ago, this scenario might have referred to thieves or robbers, or other wicked people. Does this have relevance today? Yes.

For our modern time, it could be someone asking you to invest in a movie like the example I gave. It could be someone asking you to buy a bar, or nightclub, where alcohol along with the licentious lifestyle will be promoted. It could be someone asking you to invest in a casino or movie theatre.

But Vaughn, you say, the verse talks about shedding blood. That's definitely the robbers and thieves of 2000 years ago not those modern business deals, right? Wrong. The application for today is as I have stated.

The shedding of blood is not the only physical killing or murder of a person but also the spiritual injury of a person to cause a stumbling block to be placed before them which prevents them from getting to heaven and thus dooming them to death and hell.

Let's go back to the movie example. Suppose an unwise believer invested in this movie and it became a super success. But the movie causes many people to sin against God(Yahuah). It causes them to blaspheme God(Yahuah), and lose their place in eternal life. Then that unwise believer would be accountable for their role in that "shedding of blood." You see, even though they have not physically killed a person, they were responsible in part for placing temptation or a stumbling block before them which has caused that person to stumble and fall from the path of light into the path of darkness: spiritual death!

But Vaughn, you say, if those people wanted to watch that movie, it's not my fault, so why can't I make a profit off it. Well, maybe some of those people did want to watch that and didn't love God(Yahuah) or care about God. That's their choice. But out of the millions that see that movie, what about the thousand or 10 thousand baby Christians who went to see it and lost their way? You will be held accountable for their souls because you put a stumbling block before them. And what about those non-believers who God was preparing to receive an outpouring of his blessing but they fell away upon seeing that movie. You'd be held accountable for that too.

Beloved, as a citizen of the Kingdom of Heaven, you have a responsibility to uphold the banner of truth, love, and righteousness. Yes, it means you can't invest in some of those money making opportunities. You may not be able to buy the Ferrari but at least you would not have caused anyone to stumble.

Story time: When I was a young man, I was offered the opportunity to lend my money in a venture like a Carnival show. It would mean drinking, half naked women, licentious behaviour, and a performance by Buju Banton. The promise of a nice interest on my money was the enticement plus the opportunity to be a VIP at the event. Being young and foolish, I went along with it. And all along my conscience troubled me because it was not something I would feel comfortable with. But I was a young babe in my Christian walk and did not have the knowledge of God(Yahuah) and the Kingdom of Heaven that I have today. On the day of the event, I took my uncle Rawle down with me to see the event.

It is to my shame and embarrassment that I cast my lot in with such a thing. I can only pray for the forgiveness and mercy of my God(Yahuah) for my part in such a thing.

Now I am not saying I have anything against Buju Banton, or the organizer of that event, or the people involved. I am saying it is something that is opposite my nature as a member of the Kingdom of Heaven. If I got another opportunity to be in something like that, or to be involved in a movie project that goes against my conscience, or anything of that nature, I'd have to turn it down.

Businesses like owning a tobacco company, or alcohol company, or nightclub, casino/lotto, or other businesses that lead people to sin is off the table for the believer.

Proverbs 12:6   Luke 6:22   Psalms 141:3-4
Proverbs 4:14-17   Proverbs 24:1-2 Proverbs 24:19-20
Proverbs 1:10-16

Summarize the key message of the bible verses in your own words in the space provided:

_____

_____

_____

_____

_____

_____

When you enter bad business arrangements, you endanger your relationship with God(Yahuah), and can cause the manifestation of the Poverty CURSE in your life.

Relationship To Strangers

The relationship to strangers is important for you in your spiritual walk. Do you interact with strangers that you meet with compassion or contempt? It is with love or neglect?

Jesus(Yahusha) used a parable to show the example of love toward the stranger. He told the story of the good Samaritan. The believer heading to Jerusalem then being attacked by thieves and left for dead at the side of the road was a person having a POVERTY CURSE moment. It was also a moment to present an opportunity to test the heart of three individuals.

Then a pastor or priest came walking by and when he saw the fellow, he crossed to the other side of the road and continued walking. Later on a Levite, a fellow believer, came by saw the man and crossed the road and kept on going. Lastly, a Samaritan man, who the Jews did not associate with in Jesus' day, came by. He saw this Jewish believer left for dead on the road. Instead of treating the stranger with scorn because of how they regard him, the Samaritan went and tended to the man, and took him to an inn, where he paid for the innkeeper to take care of the person. The Samaritan also promised to pay any extra expenses upon his return journey.

When Jesus(Yahusha) asked, which one had been a neighbour to his fellow man? The answer was the Samaritan. Then Jesus(Yahusha) commands us to go and do likewise. The command is to help the suffering stranger in need of compassion without regard to race, religion, skin colour, accent, or any other criteria.

God (Yahweh) commands us in the Holy Scripture, "Love ye therefore the stranger; for ye were strangers in the land of Egypt; I am the Lord your God." And again it is written, "If a stranger sojourn with thee in your land, ye shall not vex him. But the stranger that dwelleth with you shall be unto you as one born among you, and thou shalt love him as thyself" (Leviticus 19:33-34) When a person is not spiritually or mentally mature and stuck in the POVERTY CURSE, they are unable to bring themselves to help the stranger as Jesus(Yahusha) commanded.

Relationship To Enemies

Do you know that there is way in the Bible to have a relationship with your enemies? Yes, the Bible has lots of different ways in which believers have had dealings with their enemies in the past. These stories are left to show both the good and the bad.

Let's first start with God(Yahuah) and the devil, Satan. Satan is the enemy of God. Because of Satan, also known as the dragon and the serpent, there was war in the kingdom of heaven and Satan caused 1/3 of the angels of the kingdom of heaven to be exiled to earth along with himself.

Military strategy or war strategy teaches to kill your enemy but God(Yahuah) let the devil and his fallen angels live. God(Yahuah) demonstrated mercy in that case.

Revelation 12:7-9   Isaiah 14:12

Summarize the key message of the bible verses in your own words in the space provided:

_____

_____

_____

_____

_____

_____

And there are more examples of how we as modern day believers of God (Yahweh) should have a good relationship with our enemies.

In one Bible event, an army surrounded a town to capture a prophet of God(Yahuah). By the power of God, Elisha, the man of God was able to blind the entire army and take them captive. When he took them to the king of Israel, Elisha prayed for their sight to be returned and the Syrian army received their sight. But now the tables were turned. They saw they were now completely surrounded by the army of Israel. The king of Israel asked Elisha the prophet if he should kill the foreign army. Elisha told the king no. He told him, these are my prisoners and my desire is for you to feed them and let them go unharmed. An entire army was captured by one man serving God(Yahweh) only to demonstrate the mercy and love of God(Yahweh) by feeding them and letting them go free. You can read the story in 2 Kings 6: 13-23.

Jesus(Yahusha) taught the true principle of love which we as modern day believers are to reflect in our lives. In the book of Matthew (5:43-45), Jesus says:

> *Ye have heard that it hath been said, Thou shalt love thy neighbour, and hate thine enemy. But I say unto you, Love your enemies, bless them that curse you, do good to them that hate you, and pray for them which despitefully use you, and persecute you; That ye may be the children of your Father which is in heaven: for he maketh his sun to rise on the evil and on the good, and sendeth rain on the just and on the unjust.*

This is the modern day teaching that believers should follow. Today, we have people in the world who are so angry that they name, shame, and flame anyone who offends them.

Sometimes believers who should know better get caught up in the moment and behave the same way. This is not right. God (Yahuah) expects us to uplift a higher standard as a light in the darkness.

In Proverbs 16:7 the Bible says, "When a man's ways please the LORD(YAHUAH), he maketh even his enemies to be at peace with him."

In Proverbs 24:17 the Bible says, "Rejoice not when thine enemy falleth, and let not thine heart be glad when he stumbleth"

Here's a personal story I wish to share with you.

In my lifetime, I have seen my enemies suffer. God (Yahuah) has allowed me to see destruction come upon my enemies time and time again. That's why I tried not to be an enemy with people and try to live at peace with folks. One time a business associate burned me on a business deal and he owed me money. I asked him to pay and even travelled abroad to meet him and speak to him. But he was in denial. So I took the matter to the court of heaven and left it there.

Later on, I was told his relationship with his son was damaged. He and his son were fighting all the time and his son didn't want to have anything to do with him. The year after that his business burned down but thankfully his equipment was salvaged so he could startup with minimal loss. The third year, his longtime girlfriend died suddenly of a curable disease. In three years, he had three terrible tragedies in his life. I was flabbergasted by this news because I had not been giving him much thought. A non-believer might say he was unlucky or someone else might say he got Karma. I don't believe in coincidences or luck or karma.

I lodged my complaint in the court of the kingdom of heaven and he was reaping what he sowed. I contacted him and attempted to reason with him as I was genuinely concerned for his well-being. I pleaded with him to simply do right by me because I am afraid that something worst might happen to him. His reply was scathing and he accused me of the nastiest intention and called me names. I was not rejoicing in his suffering. I was genuinely concerned about his misfortune and wanted to warn him to avert any further things. Yet, his heart was hard because he idolized money more than righteousness.

My story above is one of the **Justice of Yahuah**. Those who align themselves with the enemy of the kingdom will face judgement in this world or the next one.

Now I'll share with you the **Mercy of Yahuah**. My wife is a nurse. One time in the operating room (OR) there was something going wrong with a patient and the patient was flat-lining. Immediately everybody in the room jumped into action as all their training had prepared them. They were doing the CPR. They did the shocks to restart the heart. They were all working away trying to revive the dead patient. Now according to procedure, there is a timekeeper who keeps track of how long they are trying to revive a dead patient.

After about 30 minutes or 45 minutes of trying, everyone on the room will agree that they could not revive the patient and the patient will be pronounced dead. My wife was in the room monitoring the patient's vital signs on the monitor.

The machine was flatline. After a long time, there was no result. Remember, the timekeeper is counting the time before they all have to stop. Everyone is tense. Nothing seems to be working. They are all trying their best to revive the dead patient. The doctor begins to be sad and anxious about how can they possibly explain this death to the family. The patient was still so young. My wife saw the signs that people were ready to give up. Nothing seemed to be working. Now remember the patient has been dead (no heartbeat) all this time the professionals are working to try to revive them. My wife sees the situation and walks over the patient's foot and touches their foot and prays to Yahuah to return their spirit back to them and bring them back to life.

As she finishes her prayer, there is a blip on the monitor. She gets back and tells everyone in the room the patient is alive. The mood immediately changes from despair to joy. The patient is alive. The patient is not out of the woods yet but they are alive which is a whole lot better than dead. In the middle of everything my wife says "Thank God" for saving the patient. Yahuah had revived the dead patient and that family would not suffer the loss of their loved one that day. Praise Yahuah.

My wife's story is an example of the **Mercy of Yahuah**.

My wife and are I one flesh, joined together in marriage by Yahuah. Thus, in us, you see the example of the Justice and Mercy of Yahuah joined together in our stories. This can help you understand that justice and mercy dwells with Yahuah. It is Yahuah's will that we should be married as our lives demonstrate the working of Yahuah as a life lived in faith.

Here's a key note here. The world is filled with spiritual forces, from the citizens of heaven (angels) and from the exiles of the kingdom of heaven (demons). Humans exist in a place where we are material beings but can interact with spiritual forces. When you take your prayer to the court of kingdom of heaven, it is a serious matter with far reaching consequences. It can open up CURSES in a person's life if they are wrong. It can also bring wonderful BLESSINGS into many lives. When you find a sincere god-fearing person, stick close to them.

Do your best not to be enemies with folks but also let them know your father in heaven is your defender if they choose to do wickedly. Warm them to choose good and not evil, life and not death.

In Proverbs 25:21 the Bible says, "If thine enemy be hungry, give him bread to eat; and if he be thirsty, give him water to drink:"

In Romans 12:20 the Bible says, "Therefore if thine enemy hunger, feed him; if he thirst, give him drink:"

Summarize the key message in your own words below:

_____

_____

_____

_____

_____

_____

Can you do this in your own life? Yes. If you are a believer, you can follow this principle to help show others the love of God in your life. Even non-believers have employed this method for some success to win others to their cause.

For example, the Toronto Pig Save (TPS) group, a non-religious animal rights group, is against slaughterhouses and would like to see them closed down. Thus, there is animosity between slaughterhouse workers and TPS activists. Yet, the TPS groups have told slaughters workers that they don't want workers fired. They know sometimes people take that kind of job because they need to pay their bills and have no choice. But TPS wants the end of cruelty in slaughterhouses. And some slaughterhouse workers have been touched and have quit the job or stopped eating meat or made decisions to reduce meat in their diet.
Where they would be considered enemies in the beginning, compassion and love won them over for the TPS side.

Believers of God (Yahweh) should be inclined to demonstrate love in such a capacity when fighting against social injustice. Both the old testament and new testament have the instructions for us to deal well with our enemies.

Relationship to Truth

There are 244 references to the word truth in the Bible. We live in an age where people choose to believe that truth is relative. They mistakenly believe that your truth is true for you while my truth is true for me, even though those points may be polar opposites. One must be false if the other is to be true. Hence people say things like you be you and I'll be me.

In our modern society we have a broken relationship with truth. That fractured relationship began several decades ago until now we have ended up with the broken relationship. In a world where lies are pleasant to the ears and conscience, truth is ridiculed, shouted down, labelled politically incorrect, *-phobic, or just downright mean.

Where did we begin to lose a love for the truth?

I suspect, it was when parents in the early days of television decided to let the TV become the nanny of their children. Cleverly devised fables and stories became more enticing than the love of plain and simple truths. Nanny TV stimulated the senses and the imagination with all sorts of interesting things which were not of God(Yahweh) or the kingdom of heaven.

Take one of my favourite shows when I was a boy: Mission Impossible. The characters were spies or agents who were trained to accomplish their mission using deception, misinformation, theft, or any means necessary. Then there are movies like James Bond, the spy series about an alcoholic, womanizing man who lies and kills to save the world from evil villains.

Where else has truth been replaced with something else?

How about in schools? The Bible used to be part of the instruction for children but is out of schools today. How about in colleges and universities where ancient scriptural truths have been lightly regarded and modern philosophies are taught to our young people? Is it any wonder that people graduate from these institutions without a moral compass thus contributing to the destruction of our planet?

Truth is like light. It illuminates everything it touches. Lies are like darkness. Darkness cannot be measured whereas light can be measured. Darkness is the absence of light.

Truth, like gravity, is not relative. It stands on its own. It defends itself. It crushes the darkness of lies.

God(Yahuah) is truth. In him there are no lies. The devil, Satan, is the father of lies. He is the great deceiver in the world. Jesus(Yahusha) described the devil in John 8:44, *"Ye are of your father the devil, and the lusts of your father ye will do. He was a murderer from the beginning, and abode not in the truth, because there is no truth in him. When he speaketh a lie, he speaketh of his own: for he is a liar, and the father of it."*

The more a person clings to truth (light), the more repulsive the lies (darkness) becomes to them. Likewise, the more a person clings to darkness, the more repulsive the light becomes to them.
It is impossible for light and darkness to dwell equally in the same person. Where the light is full, there can be no darkness and where there is darkness in full, there is no light.

What then is truth?

The scripture teaches us that truth is one of the traits of God (Yahweh). He is light. He is truth. In Exodus, he is described as abundant in goodness and truth. In Deuteronomy God(Yahuah) is described as perfect, just, a God of truth, and without iniquity. Psalms tells us he is a God of Truth. His works are done in truth. His light and truth leads others. He is plentiful in mercy and truth. Mercy and truth is before his face. His truth endures for all generations. His truth reaches up to the clouds.

The law [of God (Yahuah)] is the truth. All his commandments are truth. His counsels of old are faithfulness and truth. Truth therefore is absolute and unchanging.

Exodus 34:6	Deut 32:4	Psalm 43:3
Psalm 31:5	Psalm 33:4	Psalm 86:15
Psalm 100:5	Psalm 119:142	Psalm 119:151

Summarize the key message in your own words below:

_____

_____

_____

_____

_____

_____

What instructions are we given concerning truth?

The truth must be an integral part of the life of the believer. Believers are advised to serve God (Yahweh) in truth with your whole heart. Let the words of your mouth be truth. Speak truth in your heart. Bind truth around your neck and write truth on the table of your heart. Follow God (Yahweh) into truth. Keep his covenant and testimonies in truth. Walk in the truth of God (Yahweh). Cherish truth and know wisdom. Let God's truth be your shield. Judge according to truth. Call upon God(Yahweh) in truth. Acknowledge he made the heaven and earth, and sea, and all thing in them, and he keeps truth forever.

1 Samuel 12:24	1 King 17:24	Psalm 26:3
Psalm 15:2	Psalm 25:5	Psalm 51:6
Psalm 86:11	Psalm 91:4	Psalm 96:13
Psalm 145:18	Psalm 146:6	Proverb 3:3

Summarize the key message in your own words below:

_____

_____

_____

_____

_____

_____

_____

_____

What benefits are attributed to truth?

The benefits of truth include the ability to show or display righteousness. Truthful lips will be established forever. Mercy and truth purge iniquity. Mercy and truth preserve the king. People are supposed to speak truth to their fellow humans. Judging with truth and justice will bring peace to your places of authority. Truth brings persons into the light. The truth can make a person free. It exposes liars and deceivers. It helps purify the soul by obedience to truth.

Proverb 8:7	Proverb 12:17	Proverb 12:19
Proverbs 16:6	Proverbs 20:28	Zechariah 8:16
John 3:21	John 4:24	John 8:32
John 14:17	John 15:26	Ephesians 4:25
1 Peter 1:22	1 John 2:4	1 John 3:18

Summarize the key message in your own words below:

_____

_____

_____

_____

_____

_____

_____

Relationship To Those In Authority (Civil)

The Believer is taught to hold those in authority in high regard and to show them all due respect. The scripture teaches in Romans 13:1-5 that God (Yahweh) has ordained leaders (kings, heads of government, etc) to be in such powerful positions. Those who fight against such are fighting against the will of God (Yahweh). The scripture tells us that such rulers are not a terror to good works but to evil works.

When rulers do wrong, we ought to stand up to speak out against oppression but we are to also remain respectful to those doing the will of God(Yahuah) for a season. The only time we are advised to disobey leaders is in respect to matters of worship of God (Yahuah), his laws, statutes, and commandments.

Any civil power that attempts to mislead or compel the believer to worship any other god contrary to the worship of Yahuah, or attempts to restrict the worship of God(Yahweh), or attempt to dictate that you must worship God(Yahweh) but only how and when they say you can, then that rule is contrary to God(Yahuah) and is not to be followed.

Let's look at the prophet Daniel. In the book of Daniel, chapter 6, we see the ministers (presidents and princes) of the government of the Persian king Darius. They hated Daniel because he was a true servant of God (Yahuah), a faithful man, and an honest man. King Darius liked Daniel. The ministers hatched a plan to trap Daniel but they could find nothing to accuse Daniel of. They persuaded the King to pass a law forbidding anyone to pray to any god or worship any god for 30 days AND to only pray to King Darius during that time if they desired anything of a god: A civil law that attempted to dictate worship. Those jealous ministers knew that Daniel would continue to worship God (Yahuah) as was his custom for years.

Daniel loved and served his King well but Daniel could not obey an unrighteous law that attempted to dictate worship. Daniel worshiped God(Yahuah) as was his custom and the wicked and jealous ministers went straight to the king. They told the king that Daniel was disobeying the law which forbids worship to any deity but the king. And those wicked ministers wanted Daniel thrown into the lions den.

When King Darius heard this he was terribly distraught. Remember, King Darius loved Daniel. He spent all day trying to find a loophole to get Daniel off but the law was unbreakable, even for the king. He was knocking himself for being duped into this situation. Sadly, that evening, king Darius called Daniel to him and told Daniel that he would have to throw him to the lions according to the law. But Darius also said he was hoping that Daniel's God (Yahuah) would save him.

Daniel obeyed the punishment of the law. He did not try to run away and hide. Daniel was still subject to the king. He remained obedient to the king as God (Yahuah) desires.

Know what happened? It was evening when they threw Daniel into the lions den and King Darius fasted all night. He didn't sleep. He was reaching out to God (Yahuah) for Daniel. Early in the morning King Darius rushed to the lions den and sheepishly called out, "Daniel, are you okay?"

Daniel answered him that he was indeed okay and that God (Yahuah) had closed up the mouth of the lions. King Darius was delighted. His mistake had been covered over by God(Yahuah) because of love and faith. Daniel had faith. The king had love. Then the king ordered Daniel to be taken out of the lions den. The penalty had been paid.

For the treachery of the ministers, the king had them and their families thrown into the lions den. The lions were fasting all night so they were hungry when these ministers and their families were thrown in. The lions ate them up.

In our modern day life, we will have leaders who God (Yahuah) has allowed to become leaders because He has a purpose for them to fulfill.

As a believer, we have to maintain a relationship in truth, in integrity, and in holiness. We are to serve our rulers humbly as our service to God(Yahweh) as long as that service does not violate the rules of the Kingdom of God (Yahuah). The rules of God's eternal kingdom supercede the rules of human temporary kingdoms.

Note that God(Yahuah) did give us clues on how to select leaders where we have an electoral process. In Exodus 18:21 it is written, "Moreover thou shalt provide out of all the people **able men, such as fear God, men of truth, hating covetousness**; and place such over them, **to be rulers** of thousands, and rulers of hundreds, rulers of fifties, and rulers of tens."

When true and good leaders are appointed, the Poverty CURSE is greatly minimized and ALL the people prosper.

Relationship To False Prophets/Preachers

God(Yahuah) has always desired to create a nation of priests who are representatives of the Kingdom of Heaven. The nation of Israel was supposed to be that but they failed time and time again. Ordinary men and women like you and me were supposed to be evangelists of the Holy scriptures. They failed and we fail on many occasions. The relationship between you and your spiritual guide/mentor is important. These are to you like preachers and prophets.

What do the things they convey to you do to your relationship with truth, God, and all your other relationships?

Think of it. These days with social media it is so easy to be influenced by nasty, horrible things that friends or others paste on facebook that appear on your timeline. For example, I once saw a very rude and sexual Christmas cartoon on facebook. Someone posted it saying it was funny.

I looked at it and it was anything but funny. It was just sex and violence in a cartoon form with elves and Santa Clause. Once I saw that I can't unsee it. I would never have opted to watch it had there been a proper warning. I shudder to think of teens or children on facebook who might click on that "cartoon" and have their young minds negatively influenced.

Now there are preachers and teachers who should be teaching people the truth of the Kingdom of God(Yahuah), the truth about the exiles of the Kingdom of Yahuah, Satan and the devils, and the truth about separating the clean from the unclean. Yet, some of those preachers and teachers are false prophets because they don't teach the truth about any of the three areas I just mentioned.

By the errors in their doctrine, they are actually stealing the love of God(Yahuah) out of the hearts of sincere people. God says this in Jeremiah 23:23-27, "Am I a God at hand, saith Yahuah, and not a God afar off? Can any hide himself in secret places that I shall not see him? saith Yahuah. Do not I fill heaven and earth? saith Yahuah. I have heard what the prophets said, that prophesy lies in my name, saying, I have dreamed, I have dreamed. How long shall this be in the heart of the prophets that prophesy lies? yea, they are prophets of the deceit of their own heart; Which think to cause my people to forget my name by their dreams which they tell every man to his neighbour, as their fathers have forgotten my name for Baal."

You see, the people were being deceived by the spiritual leaders among them. Those wicked spiritual leaders mingled truth with error, and the vain imaginations of their heart. Those false prophets were actually causing the people to forget the true name of God (Yahuah) by including elements of worship of the exiles of the Kingdom of Yahuah (the devil/Satan/Baal/Nimrod/Pan).

False prophets have arisen all over. They spring up like weeds and attempt to deceive kings, rulers, governors, and ordinary people.

What is the ordinary, humble person seeking a true relationship with God(Yahuah) supposed to do?

The scriptures themselves give you the criteria to assess the qualification of a person to be in a position of spiritual leadership in your life. All mentors, coaches, anyone held in high regard, and spiritual leaders are to be tested against the scriptures to see if they measure up to the heavenly standard of uprightness.

Why is this necessary? Because you are trusting these persons to advise you in your everyday life in matters which can affect this life and your afterlife. The reward is eternity in heaven or eternal hell fire. Thus it is important to be sure of this relationship and to be certain that it is one in truth, righteousness, and love.

False prophets, teachers, preachers, mentors, leaders, spiritualists, etc, will lead you down the wrong path while causing you to be further ensnared by the POVERTY Curse. And while you are sinking deeper into the pit, they tell you that you're not doing it right, you need to give more, buy more, degrade yourself more, or do something contrary to the truth found in the Holy Scriptures. They know that as your situations worsens and you become more desperate, you will be more inclined to delve deeper into sin and lawlessness.

How do you spot these false prophets? One criteria given in the scripture is found in Isaiah 8:20, "To the Torah and to the Testimony! If they do not speak according to this Word, it is because there is no light to them!"

And in Jeremiah 44:23 it says, "Because ye have burned incense, and because ye have sinned against Yahuah, and have not obeyed the voice of Yahuah, nor walked in his law, nor in his statutes, nor in his testimonies; therefore this evil is happened unto you, as at this day."

The false teachers in your life lack the light of God(Yahuah) in them because they despise his laws, his statutes, his testimonies, and his commandments. They are liars and deceivers, and wolves in sheep's clothing. They want you to forget the name of God(Yahuah). Once you have identified the false prophets/preachers/teachers, avoid them and find true preachers and cling to them to avoid the POVERTY Curse.

Deuteronomy 4:45	Deuteronomy 6:17
1 Kings 2:3	2 Chronicles 34:31
Psalms 25:10	Psalms 93:5
Psalms 78:56	Psalms 119:2
Psalm 119 (all of it)	Revelation 14:2

Balaam was one of those false prophets because even though he spoke with God (Yahuah), Balaam wanted to do his own thing. When a king wanted to hire him to CURSE God's people, God(Yahuah) told him not to do it. But Balaam refused to accept it and so went with the king to CURSE God's people. Funny thing is, when he tried to pronounce the CURSE only a blessing came out of his mouth. Who God(Yahuah) has blessed, no one can CURSE. And who God (Yahuah) curses, no one can save. Read Balaam's story in Numbers 22:4 to 24:1 and Numbers 31:8,16. Balaam started out with a relationship with God(Yahuah) but he lost his way and eventually betrayed God's people and later died.

Summarize the key message of the scripture verses in your own words below:

_____

_____

_____

_____

_____

_____

_____

_____

_____

Relationship To Holiness

The numerous points of influence in our lives have done much to separate us from the life of holiness. The broken relationship to holiness keeps us separated from a full relationship with God(Yahuah). We see in the design of the mitre or crown that Aaron, the priest wore, the words HOLINESS TO THE LORD or rather HOLINESS TO YAHUAH were to be engraved. Why? This holiness is to be found in the head, and more specifically at the front of the head. Holiness is the mark of your forehead (conscious mind).

What is Holiness to God(Yahuah) and why is it important? Holiness is a state of being clean, separate, and distinct from the rest of the world. As believers of God(Yahuah), we are called to be holy in our daily lives.

Being separate in regard to holiness is not saying to go live secluded away from the world in a monastery. It is about being separate in habits and in conduct. The way to describe it would be like an ambassador of a country situated in another country. That ambassador is separate from the country where his embassy is located yet he is among the people of that country and is expected to carry himself with the deportment which the position demands. As a believer, you are to become an ambassador of the Kingdom of God(Yahuah).

I ask you then, should a true Christian believer be following the things of the world so that they become indistinguishable from the world? No. This is not holiness. This is conformity to the world.

Back in the time of Daniel and the three Hebrew companions, we see in the book of Daniel, chapter 3, the king built a huge golden statue. He commanded all the people of his kingdom to bow to the statute at a certain hour according to his design.

There were three Hebrews who were Holy Unto Yahuah among the gathering. They were separate from the world in which they lived yet were present in the world. Their uniqueness was undeniable. They had been set apart from the kingdom of Nebuchadnezzar, and were shining lights of the Kingdom of God(Yahuah). They were like lighthouses.

It may not have been an easy thing for them. It may have caused friction at times. But if you read the very beginning of their story, you can see they purposed in their heart to remain holy. Also, in the story of Daniel chapter 3, you see how mighty God(Yahuah) worked in their lives. Blessings were poured out from heaven. These 3 men were beyond the Poverty CURSE. Read the wonderful miracle that happened because they were Holy. Should a believer of God(Yahuah) be cussing and swearing, drinking alcohol, or getting tattoos, or following the latest fashion trends, or other devices of this world? No. It is the pursuit of these things that are causing many to manifest a broken relationship with God(Yahuah). God(Yahuah) says that we should be holy as he is holy.

There is also a considerable amount of peer pressure to be like everyone else. People don't like the discomfort of feeling they stick out like a sore thumb. From kindergarten, children are taught to be like their peers. They are to sit politely like their peers, take breaks with their peers, show up for school, and leave school like their peers. This is continued all the way up to university where youth finally get to express some of their individuality. After 15-20 years of social programming to be like everyone else, it is easy to understand why changing can be a challenge. However it is not impossible and people do become BORN AGAIN all the time.

Remember, when the world see no difference between you and itself, then you are not living up to the standard and banner of being Holy Unto Yahuah. You need to live out holiness daily in your life, in your thoughts, your actions, your words, and your deeds. You are to show others that the God(Yahuah) that you serve is greater that the temporal things of this world.

Story time: In my earlier days, I was a bit of a travelling seeker visiting churches to see how they worship God. Over the years, I visited many churches and observed the way the people in the church speak, dress, and behave.

The manner in which they conduct themselves speaks volumes to me about their relationship to God(Yahuah) and their efforts to live a holy life. If I see the children and teenagers of the congregation behaving in an unrestrained and lawless manner during their free time, then it tells me that the parents are failing to educate their children properly.

If I see the females of the church dressing immodestly, then I know they are not fully on the path of holiness. If I listen to the manner in which the members of the congregation speak, I can hear worldliness or holiness in their words. I remember being in one church and wondering how can the elders not see the condition of the children. Don't they see their youth are in danger of having minds fashioned for the work of the Satan, the exile of the Kingdom of God(Yahuah)? The children were unruly and undisciplined.

The scripture is true when it suggests that you can know a person by their fruit.

It can be difficult because of a lifetime of bad habits you have built up. However, being holy is possible when you make the decision in your mind to be holy and you learn and follow the guidelines to help separate you from the unholiness found in the world.

1 Chronicles 16:29	Exodus 28:36
Leviticus 19:2	2 Chronicles 31:18
Psalm 29:2	Psalm 95:5
Isaiah 63:18	Jeremiah 2:3
Luke 1:74-75	Romans 6:18-22
Acts 3:12	2 Corinthians 7:1
Ephesians 4:22-27	Titus 2:1-8
Leviticus 11:44-45	1 Thessalonians 4:7
Numbers 15:40	Leviticus 20:26
1 Corinthians 7:34	Ephesians 1:3-4
Revelation 22:10-12	

Summarize the key message of the scripture verses in your own words below:

_____

_____

_____

_____

_____

_____

_____

Relationship To Order and Chaos

This point came up because of a very thought provoking article I read by Mallory Millett entitled "Marxist Feminism Ruined Lives." Mallory was the sister of a very prominent leader in the marxist feminist movement. Mallory wrote:

It was 1969. Kate invited me to join her for a gathering at the home of her friend, Lila Karp. They called the assemblage a "consciousness-raising-group," a typical communist exercise, something practiced in Maoist China. We gathered at a large table as the chairperson opened the meeting with a back-and-forth recitation, like a Litany, a type of prayer done in Catholic Church. But now it was Marxism, the Church of the Left, mimicking religious practice:

"Why are we here today?" she asked.
"To make revolution," *they answered.*
"What kind of revolution?" she replied.
"The Cultural Revolution," *they chanted.*
"And how do we make Cultural Revolution?" she demanded.
"By destroying the American family!" *they answered.*
"How do we destroy the family?" she came back.
"By destroying the American Patriarch," *they cried exuberantly.*
"And how do we destroy the American Patriarch?" she replied.
"By taking away his power!"
"How do we do that?"
"By destroying monogamy!" *they shouted.*
"How can we destroy monogamy?"
"By promoting promiscuity, eroticism, prostitution and homosexuality!" *they resounded.*

Now if we look around at the world we live in today, there is an abundance of promiscuity, eroticism, prostitution, etc. Average middle class men are feeling less empowered and are not fulfilling their potential. In 2016, we are reaping the fruits of seeds planted since the 1960s.

How many wives have read the books which promote this worldly and carnal philosophy and simply abandoned their husbands and children leaving the family broken and crushed? This creates deep emotional wounds in the husband, the children, and even the woman, which can take decades to heal if it ever does.

How many young ladies have chosen to give up on the notion of marriage to one man after being indoctrinated in this lifestyle? How many women have shown little to no regard for sanctity of the life of their unborn child as they killed the child in the womb? The scripture tells us that God (Yahuah) warns against hurting the child in the womb. God (Yahuah) is the one who will fight for these children.

The chant Mallory writes about listening to is a master plan to disrupt order in societal structure and create chaos. The aim of this chaos is to cause revolution and out of this revolution there is a hope to accomplish the devices of the group.

The words to one of Bob Marley's songs springs to mind: Men see their dreams and aspirations crumble in front of their face, and all of their wicked intentions to destroy the human race.

God (Yahuah) is the God of order and harmony. Is there a way for an ordinary community of believers to destroy the plan outlined by those ladies way back in 1969? Yes. The goal to destroy monogamy can easily be defeated when one remembers the commandment Thou shall not commit adultery.

Humans make plans. God (Yahuah) makes plans too. When we reject the order that God would desire for our lives then the result is chaos.

Let's just look at how orderly God(Yahuah) is in his creation. He created seven days of the week. Six days he created the world and everything in it and the seventh day he created an oasis in time. There is an order to the creation.

What about the order in the home? God (Yahuah) desires that parents teach their children how to be good and responsible stewards in the home. Children should be given age appropriate responsibilities and encouraged when they do a good job. They should be taught the importance of daily prayer, worship, fasting, exercise, nutrition, and rest. There is an order of learning and living.

When you reject order and embrace chaos, you also embrace the Poverty CURSE in your life too. Order gives assurance of a defined outcome. Order strengthens faith. Chaos is unpredictable and the outcome is always uncertain.

There are additional relationships that are impacted but I don't have space in the book for them. They are Education, Health, Forgiveness, Compassion. These are covered in the online course.

* * *

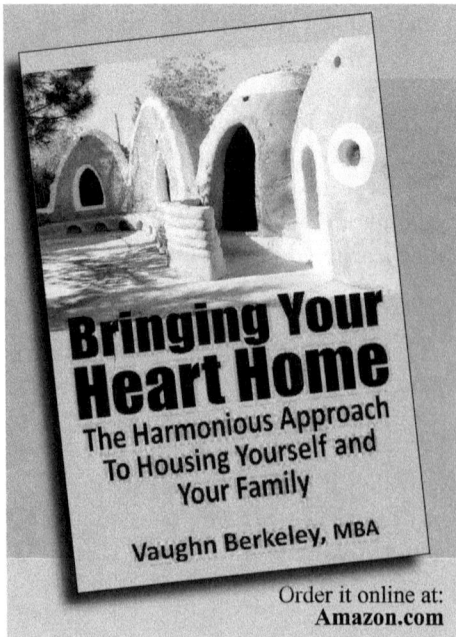

Bringing Your Heart Home
The Harmonious Approach To Housing Yourself and Your Family

Vaughn Berkeley, MBA

Order it online at:
Amazon.com

Housing is one of the areas that can be impacted by the Poverty Curse. Are you doing the things to protect yourself or to expose yourself to the CURSE? My book is one book that can help you understand the concept of housing from a biblical and practical perspective!

Course Note: This chapter introduces a principle of love and connections. Relationships should be about love but the wrong relationship brings more sorrow than joy. In this course module for this chapter, write some of the ways you can develop these relationship traits within yourself.

_____

_____

_____

_____

_____

_____

_____

_____

_____

_____

_____

* * *

Stop And Think

Don't just rush into the next chapter. We covered a lot of stuff on relationships in this chapter. It should cause you to question the relationships in your life. Examine your emotions. Why do you feel this way? Can you really become free from the CURSE?

Realization: Now I understand truly these pillars of relationships I need godliness in my life. I know that the Creator of the universe is on my side and His power is sufficient to get me out from under the CURSE. I desire to start creating godly relationships according to his will. I have taken the steps in this chapter to move forward out of the curse.

Prayer: Almighty God(Yahuah), I now understand another piece of the puzzle about how I was under the CURSE. Please forgive me for my sins and wilful disobedience of your laws concerning relationships. Teach me of you and your ways. Help me to follow you wholeheartedly. Renew my heart, my mind, my body and soul for you. Break this CURSE for your name sake. Thank you for loving me enough to intervene in my life at this present time. Please fill my life with your love and help me share all you teach me with others around me. Blessed be Yahuah, God Almighty. Amen.

Affirmation: Today I know the truth and I AM FREE.

* * *

Go to checkpoint #5:
www.breakthepovertycurse.com

* * * * *

Write Your Personal Insights Here

_____

_____

_____

_____

_____

_____

_____

_____

_____

_____

_____

* * * * *

In our course on Breaking the Poverty Curse at Berkeley Academy, we tackle the topic in more details and give you more fast start money ideas for your cash flow situation. You are simply lacking in some core aspects of fast cash seeding and reaping. Check out the course at http://berkeley.academy/our-courses/

* * * * *

Renewal Of Your Mind

Chapter 6

* * *

The blessing of the LORD, it maketh rich, and he addeth no sorrow with it. - Proverb 10:22

Maturity doesn't come with age; it comes with acceptance of responsibility. - Ed Cole

Your old thinking got you to where you are now. If you want to be somewhere else 1 year from now, you've got to change your thinking via renewing your mind. ~ Vaughn Berkeley, MBA

* * *

The Promise of Freedom

It is a serious thing when we talk about the mind. We have what we call baggage. It is the accumulation of things we have experienced in our lives up to this moment in time. It has shaped our character, our mental outlook, and to some extent, even our physical attributes. Thus, if you want radical change in your life, you are only going to get it by renewing your mind. The old mind with the old ways of thinking and seeing the world is ill equipped to take you forward in this journey.

God(Yahuah) knows about the human condition and has already made provision for us for the renewing of our minds.

Have you done a diagnosis in the Assessing the POVERTY CURSE chapter? Are you aware that you are under the CURSE?

You may not have the full extent of the CURSE upon you, so you think everything is okay, but, you should look around you and be able to read the signs much as you would read the newspaper, or look at the sky to judge the weather.

Well, I can tell you that there is good news for you. There is a promise made to set those free who desire to be free.

Here are some of the promises available to us all through the Gospel of Jesus (Yahusha):
- Someone To Bring Truth and Justice to All the Land
- Sight to the Blind
- Freedom to Prisoners (Slaves/Bondage)
- Freedom to Those in Darkness

Isaiah 42:1-9   Isaiah 61

Note the key points of each verse below:

_____

_____

_____

_____

_____

_____

We can see from the verses above that JUSTICE and RIGHT and TRUTH will be revealed to the nations. That means you, me and everyone. The promise is that this message will not fail. Man has tried to conceal, hide, burn, destroy and remove the Bible and the Gospel of Jesus(Yahusha) and has failed miserably.

It still exists today for our benefit, to help us to be free. See, there is hope. Messiah came and brought forth the truth. It is recorded in the Gospel and in the Bible. We have to search them out.

Here are some more promises:
- A QUALIFIED and APPOINTED teacher
- GOOD TIDINGS to the Meek, Poor, Afflicted
- HEALING to the Broken-hearted
- LIBERTY to (Physical and Spiritual) Captives/Slaves
- COMFORT to Mourners
- RIGHTEOUSNESS Restored
- JOY Restored
- PROSPERITY Restored
- HONOUR to replace your Shame

Now we know we have the promise of help. The way to get out of this CURSE is two-pronged. First, recognize that you are enslaved, and powerless to get out on your own. You must admit and accept, that only through the assistance of the Divine Almighty Yahuah can your life be changed.

Secondly, you have to resolve in your heart and mind to do what is necessary on your part to turn this around. This can be a hard thing to do. I'm not saying that it will be easy, but I am saying that given the alternative, wouldn't you rather be free than a slave, BLESSED rather than CURSED?

Your Responsibilities

Yes, you do have some responsibilities. Some of the things you need to do include:
- WASH Yourself (Physical and Spiritual)
- CEASE from doing all EVIL (the things which bring you under the CURSE)
- LEARN to DO RIGHT
- SEEK Justice
- RELIEVE the oppressed
- CORRECT the oppressor
- DEFEND the fatherless (orphan)
- PLEAD for the widow
- Be WILLING and OBEDIENT (in truth)

WASH Yourself (Physically and Spiritually)
We see in the Bible that Ruth, an ancestor of King David, was told by Naomi to "wash thyself therefore, and anoint thee, and put thy raiment upon thee, and get thee down to the floor: [but] make not thyself known unto the man, until he shall have done eating and drinking." Ruth 3:3(KJV)

I have seen people in the middle of turmoil simply let themselves go. They don't shave, brush their teeth, shower or take care of their physical appearance. Some people have even gone out in public smelling like urine.

It is unhealthy and degrading for you to carry yourself like this. Aside from the mental and emotional self degradation you undergo, you must also not allow yourself to become physically weakened, that you succumb to disease. This would simply be adding insult to injury.

Remember, you are created in the image of God (Yahuah). Though our physical bodies currently seem unlike celestial bodies, we have a promise that we will be transfigured when Christ (Yahusha) returns for us into a glory like His. So, keep this simple body in perfect form until the new one comes.

It is important to note that the Bible also speaks to people who wash themselves so that they appear outwardly (physically) clean and beautiful, but are inwardly (spiritually) dirty. Jeremiah 2:22 states, "'For though thou wash thee with nitre, and take thee much soap, [yet] thine iniquity is marked before me," saith the Lord GOD.'

Jesus(Yahusha) put it another way. In Matthew 23:25-28 He states, "Woe unto you, scribes and Pharisees, hypocrites! for ye pay tithe of mint and anise and cumin, and have omitted the weightier matters of the law, judgement, mercy, and faith: these ought ye to have done, and not to leave the other undone. Ye blind guides, which strain at a gnat, and swallow a camel. Woe unto you, scribes and Pharisees, hypocrites! for ye make clean the outside of the cup and of the platter, but within they are full of extortion and excess. Thou blind

Pharisee, cleanse first that which is within the cup and platter, that the outside of them may be clean also. Woe unto you, scribes and Pharisees, hypocrites! for ye are like unto whited sepulchres, which indeed appear beautiful outward, but are within full of dead men's bones, and of all uncleanness. Even so ye also outwardly appear righteous unto men, but within ye are full of hypocrisy and iniquity."

Jesus(Yahusha) was not saying that the Jewish leaders of the time were bad dishwashers and didn't know how to clean their cups and plates. He was speaking to their physical and spiritual washing. Though they looked very clean and GQ on the outside, their inner spiritual condition was one of uncleanness.

So we can see that the physical washing is only one part of the process of washing. We are after all, physical and spiritual beings and we need to wash ourselves spiritually also.

To wash yourself spiritually, you need to turn to God, Yahweh(Yahuah) and Christ(Yahusha) to wash away the pain, guilt, sin and suffering that afflicts your soul.

Talk to God (Yahweh) and confess all the thoughts of your soul to Him.

Ellen White (Christ's Object Lessons, 1900) writes:
Return to your Father's house. He invites you, saying, "Return unto Me; for I have redeemed thee." Isaiah 44:22. Do not listen to the enemy's suggestion to stay away from Christ until you have made yourself better; until you are good enough to come to God. If you wait until then, you will never come… Never a prayer is offered, however faltering, never a tear is shed, however secret, never a sincere desire after God is cherished, however feeble, but the Spirit of God goes forth to meet it. Even before the prayer is uttered or the yearning of the heart made known, grace from Christ goes forth to meet the grace that is working upon the human soul.

Wash yourself today!

- Psalms 32:1-6
- Isaiah 1:16
- Matthew 3:3-6

Note the key points of each verse below:

_____

_____

_____

_____

_____

Here's a guide to help you clean yourself.
1.   If you've never made your bath an enjoyment, then do so now. Get some nice natural scented oils and run yourself a nice bath and soak it in. Clean yourself and think of how much God enjoys your taking time to clean yourself. Bath in the morning and in the evening. Enjoy a shower too. Maybe if you're busy, you can shower in the morning and run a bath in the evening, when you have time to soak.
2.   You must undergo your spiritual bath. Simply put, you need to be baptized by water immersion, confessing your sins for their forgiveness. If you were baptized as a baby, then you probably didn't confess any sins or even think about them, so you have to be baptized again.

Now I'm not saying run out to the very first church you see and be baptized. Remember, the objective of this book is to lead you out of the Poverty CURSE. You have to be baptized no doubt, but before you make a decision about where to be baptized, pray about it earnestly. Seek God's (Yahuah) guidance, and most importantly, seek the truth. Only truth can set you free. Half of the truth is just a pretty lie. Most of all believe that God(Yahuah) will guide you to His truth, and out from the CURSE.

John the Baptist was a human washer, as opposed to a dish washer. I admire him because of how important his role was, leading up to the first advent of the Messiah, Jesus (Yahusha).

Don't miss this point! In King David's time, there was a lot of soul searching and internal turmoil, about whether or not one's sins were actually forgiven. Now we fast forward hundreds of years later, and John the Baptist gives people an assurance that their sins are forgiven by God via their confession and baptism.

Isn't it beautiful, that we can wash ourselves both physically and spiritually? Don't you feel comforted? It is wonderful to know that the God (Yahuah) who knows all, is waiting to forgive us, if we sincerely come to Him. He is the creator and restorer of our souls. Wash yourself and take a step toward Freedom from the CURSE.

CEASE from doing all EVIL

Now you may say, "I'm a good person. I am not doing any evil." You may not be a rapist or a killer, or you may not be a thief, but you should at least evaluate yourself, and stop that which is not beneficial to you. Get rid of anything which is keeping you under the Poverty CURSE! These include, but are not limited to:

LAZINESS

Proverbs 6:6-11

Have you ever considered why the Bible would send us to look at the ant? It is a tiny creature compared to us. Yet, it demonstrates a mark of character that ennobles this humble creature.

The Bible is fun the way it teases us also. To direct us to the ant, is actually telling us to get down on our knees, and look intently and with purpose at this little creature. We must now humble ourselves to consider something which we overlook in our daily living. How many times while walking on the sidewalk, do you stop just before your foot squashes an ant? Like me, you probably don't stop, because you don't even see the creature unless there are a huge number of them.

So the lesson here is to humble yourself, learn how to practise diligent and persistent work ethics, then do it. Find other diligent "ants" like yourself and work together to achieve something great! I speak more about ants in a later chapter of this book.

Ellen White (Counsels to Parents, Teachers, and Students, 1913) writes,
The path of toil appointed to the dwellers on earth may be hard and wearisome; but it is honored by the footprints of the Redeemer, and he is safe who follows in this sacred way. By precept and example, Christ has dignified useful labor… His example shows us that it is man's duty to be industrious and that labor is honorable.

Apply yourself to diligent work and take a step toward Freedom from the CURSE.

WICKEDNESS

Proverbs 17:11, 13   Luke 19:2-9

Note the key points of each verse below:

_____

_____

_____

_____

Borrowing And Not Returning (Psalms 37:21): Do you borrow things and not return them? **Stop it!** The wicked borrow and do not repay. Go and return all that you have promised to return, or at least offer something to make amends. If you were sincere, then take hope because God, Yahweh(Yahuah) knows your heart, and will give you the ability to repay as you escape the CURSE. Write your debt in a book so you will not forget, and when you are able, go and repay it.

Zacchaeus, in the book of Luke, gained assurance of his salvation from Jesus(Yahusha). Zacchaeus gave half of his goods to the poor, plus repaid four times anything he took wrongly. Yet, he is described as a rich man. To add a double blessing, Christ(Yahusha) told him that salvation was come to his house. Give to the poor and repay what you've unjustly taken or borrowed, and take a step toward Freedom from the CURSE.

Gossiping (Psalms 35:16,20): Do you gossip about others? Do you talk about people when they are not around but would never tell them how you feel to their face? **Stop it!** The Bible states, that the wicked gnash their teeth at others. Look around you and you'll see that it is true. A person with a terrible intention toward another human being gossips about that person. I could never understand how a gossip columnist is able to face him/herself, knowing that daily, their actions are killing other human beings, in the spiritual and emotional sense.

I once heard a speaker in his sermon say that he loves to gossip. Everyone was taken aback because we know gossip is wrong. Knowing that he shocked everyone he then proceeded to explain that he loves to gossip about Christ(Yahusha) not other people. Some listeners began to relax as they seemed more comfortable with that idea.

I tell you now, that gossip is equivalent to murder by the tongue, and is not permissible under any circumstances. Unfortunately the speaker's misconception of how serious an offence gossip is, led him to make an error in judgement.

This error left uncorrected, could plant a seed in the mind of the listeners, which may, years later, find gossip as acceptable. It has been said that words are cheap but the Bible says in Matthew 12:36-37 that "...by thy words thou shalt be justified, and by thy words thou shalt be condemned."

Words are therefore not cheap; they only appear deceptively so. They are like an enormous credit card bill that you don't pay now, but will ultimately pay later.

In 1 Timothy 5:13 the Bible relates that gossipers go from place to place telling things they should not tell. With our modern technology, it's more like an email, instant message, text message, or phone call, video clip, snapchat, periscope, or a social media status update. Gossiping is even done when you use your cell to video record someone in an awkward position then forward it to others or post those videos on YouTube for millions of people to watch.

Have you ever heard of a boyfriend/girlfriend breaking up and the entire world knows because they are spewing insults on facebook or twitter? We live in a society where young people lack the character <u>virtue of discretion</u>. They would rather blab about something on social media than speak to the person face to face, or even, to be humble and pray for the individual that wronged them.

It seems that people want loyalty and discretion but are incapable of it themselves these days.

Have you heard of a teenager sexting her photo to her boyfriend in trust and he forwarded the photo to a few friends then the girl's honour and reputation is ruined and she has to move to a new school because the shame is unbearable? This is a form of gossip in this new age. The naked photo was sent to the boyfriend in confidence and trust. The moment he hit the forward button, he turned into a gossiper, murdering her reputation and good name. Sexting is wrong. Gossiping is doubling the mistake. This is why we are instructed to not gossip in the Bible. God knew the damage gossip does to a person. **Stop it!**

There is another troubling thing I have noticed with social media. People will see something rude, or lewd taking place in a public setting and begin filming it with their cellphone cameras. Then they will upload this film unto YouTube for fun and entertainment of the viewers around the world. Essentially, it is gossiping about the lack of good judgement of the people involve with visual evidence to prove it. Ungodly people indulge their first instinct to want to "tell" the world this bit of juicy thing they discovered.

Stop murdering with your gossip and take a step toward Freedom from the CURSE.

Grumbling or Murmuring: This is the sister of gossiping. In gossiping you involve others. In grumbling or murmuring, you involve yourself. Do you find yourself complaining about others or something under your breath? Do you grumble about something for hours until it gets you worked up into a frenzy? Do you complain and become negative? **Stop it!** When you grumble you place yourself under the CURSE, and distance yourself from the blessing.

Grumbling is telling those around you that you are dissatisfied, and it is a form of self-complaining. You talk under your breath to yourself about something, until you get really worked up about it. It is wicked on several levels.

1.   It accuses the person(s) you are grumbling about, without giving them any chance to defend him/herself. You are judging and condemning in secret, which is wrong.

2. It is a sin because it transforms the words of your mouth into the desires of heart. So if you grumble wickedly, your heart has the potential to embrace wickedness in action.
3. It is telling God, Yahweh(Yahuah) that you don't trust Him to handle things for you.

The Bible shows us two very distinct examples of grumblers and the outcome.

In the books of Exodus 16 and Numbers 11 and 14, we see the Israelites grumbled against Moses and Aaron and even God (Yahuah). Each time some were killed by a plague or some form of judgement, yet, the others did not learn. Finally, God (Yahuah) told them that all the adults over 20 would die in the wilderness, and only their children would possess the promise land. This is how serious grumbling is in the eyes of God (Yahuah).

Another grumbler was Judas Iscariot who betrayed Jesus(Yahusha). He grumbled when Mary Magdalene poured the ointment on Jesus' feet. Of course, we later find that Judas died by hanging himself. CURSED is the person who hangs on a tree. Judas was under the CURSE though he was so close to the redeemer.

In today's society, there is so much discontentment everywhere. People are unhappy because they are not content.

Wives want the perfect husband. Husbands want wives who look like movie stars. Children want the latest toys or gadgets in the stores. Moreover, people who have not learnt how to just let stuff go, grumble about their perceived suffering, which led to their discontentment. A friend of mine disliked spending time with another person who grumbled and complained about everything. My friend said it felt like he was attending a pity-party. Grumbling affects your emotional state, your mental state, as well as your friendships and relationships. **Stop it!**

Isaiah 29:24

The prophet in Isaiah 29 suggests that you learn good doctrine instead of grumbling, and stop erring in the spirit, but get understanding. Follow the prophet's advice to lead you into the blessing, and take a step toward Freedom from the CURSE.

Mocking and Scorning: Do you mock and scornfully mistreat others who are trying to do right? **Stop it!** The wicked and ungodly mock others maliciously. The Oxford dictionary defines mocking as treating someone or something with contempt or ridicule. Whenever you do this to another human being, you are generating evil in the world, and at the same time, attaching the CURSE to yourself. People mock government, they mock each other with very little regard to its sinfulness, in today's world. Sadly, some have become quite callous and desensitized to the hurt this ridicule causes. I remember a snowboarding video game my brother played as a kid. In it, when a certain character hit a tree or fell on the course, he said, "I don't mind the pain, it's the ridicule that hurts." It was funny in the game. But ridicule does hurt humans in real life. The wound may not be physical but they hurt and sometimes that pain lasts longer than a physical hurt might last. If you want to be FREE from the CURSE make every effort to stop this.

Proverbs 1:24-26   Proverbs 14:9

Stop mocking and scorning and take a step toward Freedom from the CURSE.

Malicious Pride: Do you look at others from the tip of your nose, and think you are better than others? **Stop it!** The Bible says there is a person with teeth like a sword and knives and this person devours the poor and the needy from the earth. If you think you are better than others, and you justify yourself by putting people down and criticizing them or maligning their character, then you must stop this or you will remain in the CURSE.

I can tell you, that over the years, I've been on a few committees where some committee members felt the only way they could win, was by destroying someone else's idea, belittling them or crushing their spirit. Unfortunately those people will find themselves under the CURSE.

Proverbs 14:6   Isaiah 29:20-21

Stop malicious words and behaviour and take a step toward Freedom from the CURSE.

But Vaughn, you say, those people have the promotions, the fancy cars, or the hot young wife or husband. It does not seem like they are under the CURSE. Well, beloved, I can tell you that the Bible teaches that because God(Yahuah) seems to delay his judgement, people take it as liberty to continue on in their wicked ways. Yet their end will be utter destruction.

Story time: Years ago, while I was a young man, a client of mine was facing racial oppression in the workplace. She was being ridiculed by her boss as being stupid, not hard working, and this really made my client frustrated and sad. She was in an emotional turmoil facing undue hardship and distress. She would cry to me of her oppression and one day asked for my help.

We prayed about it and together we documented the incidents of racism she had to endure, the unjust employee evaluations she had received, and other oppressive measures. We structured the case and invoked the help of heaven.

The lady took the matter to human resources in her company and her boss has never recovered from that. The boss lost the prestige, the glory, and the management position. To this day, the "boss" is nothing like the former self.

So sometimes, our God(Yahuah) takes time before He gets into action but when he does the enemies of his children are unable to stand in that day.

Falsehood: Do you lie, cheat, or misrepresent the truth? **Stop it!** Be truthful always. If you feel like you're going to tell a lie, shut up! If you feel like cheating, do nothing! This is important on a personal level, because people are led to believe that little "white" lies are okay, because after all, they are white lies. No lies are okay. Lies are lies and are sin. Lies keep you under the CURSE. There is no distinction between a little lie and a big lie. The belief that a little lie is okay is also a lie and it has opened the way to greater lies which enslave the person under the CURSE.

Ellen White (The Ellen G. White 1888 Materials, 1888, chpt 151) writes,
"O that they had humbled their hearts in penitence and contrition! Then the divine Shekinah would have poured its precious, glorious light upon the Lord's instrumentalities, and every heart could have been made to rejoice. If they had walked in his way and kept his statutes, the Lord would have confirmed them in their position, and would have given them his grace and wisdom. Prosperity would have attended them just as long as they walked in humility, taking Christ as their pattern."

Put off falsehood and take a step toward Freedom from the CURSE.

FAILURE TO ACCEPT CORRECTION

Do you believe that most people are full of garbage so you ignore their advice? **Stop it!** Advice should be carefully weighed, and if it is good, and in accordance with God's (Yahuah) standards, then accept it and change.

If someone were to walk up to you, and tell you that you have toilet paper on your shoe, do you tell him you don't believe him and keep on walking, or do you in turn check it

out yourself? The same principle must be applied to advice.
Not all advice is good so all advice must be carefully weighed
and considered against the Bible, as the source of truth.

2 Timothy 3:16   1 Timothy 4:8-9
Proverb 12:1   Isaiah 1:17-18

Note the key points of each verse below:

_____

_____

_____

_____

_____

Do you think that there is no God (Yahuah), and no one can
tell you what to do and how to act? Do you think you are
your own best guide? **Stop it!** It is written, the fool says in
his heart there is no God.

Do you turn away from wisdom? **Stop it!** The Bible firmly
rebukes this behaviour and encourages us to learn to do well.

Perhaps you hate to be corrected, because, as a child you
were abused, chastised and berated at every opportunity by
wicked parents. Perhaps you have a spouse or sibling who
chastises you for every little thing, no matter how
insignificant. Maybe you had to write out the same sentence
hundreds of times as penance/correction for a school
infraction. So now your concept of correction is warped by
these abuses. Well, they were abuses, and you will now have
a true understanding of correction.

Ellen White (Child Guidance, 1954) writes:

The true object of reproof is gained only when the wrongdoer himself is led to see his fault and his will is enlisted for its correction. When this is accomplished, point him to the source of pardon and power.

Thus correction is a two way street not a one way. It is a partnership to be engaged in between the corrector and the wrongdoer. It should give the wrongdoer a sense of empowered hope, because there is help to become better. It should be seen as a way to escape the CURSE. However sometimes the person doing the correcting is no better at solving the problem like two alcoholics drinking together and one turns to his buddy and says alcohol is bad for you and you should stop. If the advice is biblically sound but the helper is not there then don't be afraid to take the advice and look elsewhere for help. Be persistent.

Accept righteous correction and take a step toward Freedom from the CURSE.

GREED

Did you see the 80's movie Wall Street? The main character, Gordon Gekko, played by Michael Douglas, is driven by an insatiable greed.

I remember when I was younger I admired his speech on greed, but now I know better. In his speech he said "Greed is good, greed is right. It cuts through, clarifies and focuses." The movie did depict that the final result of all this greed, was the destruction of lives, and the loss of one's dignity and honour.

The reality is, greed is not good. Greed, in all its forms, has been responsible for the death and destruction, and pain and suffering of countless people through all the ages.

Ezekiel 22:12-14   Proverbs 30:15-16
Galatians 5:19-21

Note the key points of each verse below:

_____

_____

_____

_____

_____

Do you have an insatiable desire for things, be it food, drink, fun, sex, money, cars, thrills, or anything earthly? **Stop it!** This does not mean that there is no hope for you. In Christ, there is always hope for you. Do you feel like you have no control over your thoughts and motives? **Stop it!**

The Bible lists the works of the carnal man, including adultery, fornication, uncleanness, lasciviousness, idolatry, witchcraft, hatred, variance, emulations, wrath, strife, seditions, heresies, envy, murders, drunkenness, revellings, and such things. Greed and selfishness, are at the root of these things. In Christ's strength you can overcome.

Do you think you can take and take, until you own it all? **Stop it!** The Bible asks us to consider what profit is it if a man gain the whole world and lose his soul. The cost of uncontrolled greed is too great.

Ellen White(Christ's Object Lessons, 1900) writes,
As the Lord's vineyard they were to produce fruit altogether different from that of the heathen nations. These idolatrous peoples had given themselves up to work wickedness. Violence and crime, greed, oppression, and the most corrupt practises, were indulged without restraint. Iniquity, degradation, and misery were the fruits of the corrupt tree. In marked contrast was to be the fruit borne on the vine of God's planting... In the purity of their characters, in the holiness of their lives, in their mercy and loving-kindness and compassion,

they were to show that "the law of the Lord is perfect, converting the soul." Psalm 19:7.

But you say, that you have all the wealth a man could desire in this world, so obviously, you're not under any CURSE of poverty. Look again. You can be poor in health, poor in education, poor in any number of ways including the most important, poor spiritually.

Don't let the presence of money blind you to the other CURSES of poverty in your life. Now that I have told you all of this, you must choose for yourself. You must choose to put away greed. If you make the choice in your mind and your heart, and you say it with your mouth, you will have taken another step out from under the CURSE.

Put away greed and take a step toward Freedom from the CURSE.

DISOBEDIENCE

Do you have a spirit of rebellion and reject the wise and good things you have learnt? **Stop it!** The Bible teaches us that disobedience to righteousness is a terrible sin. If you do this, then you align yourself with the wicked and are counted among them. You will surely fall under the CURSE.

1 Samuel 15:23   Proverbs 17:11
Galatians 5:19-21

Note the key points of each verse below:

_____

_____

_____

_____

Do you think that your father is full of garbage and your mother is almost useless? **Stop it!** The Bible teaches that if you mock and scoff at your father, and hate to obey your mother, the birds will pick out your eyes. This may not be literal but in a symbolic sense. If you don't have your eyes then you will be blind. If you are blind then how can you see in this life. You may suffer from emotional or spiritual blindness as a result of mistreating your sincere believing parents.

This does not give your parents carte blanche over your life. It does mean that you are to weigh their advice carefully and judge wisely. If the advice is not sound then respectfully decline it. Above all, treat your parents with respect and love. They may be under the CURSE, and need you to help them out of it.

Do you know something about God(Yahuah), but find his ways too difficult to obey? **Stop it!** The Bible says, "God says, 'All day long I stood ready to accept people who disobey and are stubborn.'" The Bible also says, "If you are willing and obedient, you shall eat the good of the land; But if you refuse and rebel, you will be devoured by the sword. For the mouth of the Lord has spoken it."

Isaiah 65:2   Isaiah 1:19-20

Note the key points of each verse below:

_____

_____

_____

_____

_____

Carefully consider this point. Yahuah, God, the creator of all things that are made is waiting on you. The Creator of everything you see, hear, feel and touch, is waiting on you to accept Him. He wants to rescue you from a world under attack by wicked forces. If you would only heed his advice and obey, you could avoid the dangers. His laws are not meant to be harmful or difficult or even stressful. It's exactly the opposite. They are meant to bring peace of mind and comfort. For example, the Bible teaches that the righteous will never be forsaken, nor their seed beg for food. This can give the obedient, righteous person great peace of mind.

The Bible also teaches that people should honour their mother and father. This is great comfort for any parent. It means that when the parent gets older, they should not be thrown away by their children as useless items, but cared for. The Bible teaches that people should not kill (murder). In countries where people disregard this law, we see how unsafe the place becomes, and how peace of mind is shattered. My mother once told me about a friend of hers. Her friend lives in a house with bars on all the doors and windows, because of her concern about crime. My mother's friend once remarked that she was living in the prison while the criminals were free to roam as they want. This is exactly the mindset that develops when society disregards the sacred rules.

Learn obedience to the right way and take a step toward Freedom from the CURSE.

SELFISHNESS

Do you think only of yourself? Do you think that you're the greatest gift to mankind, and you're not afraid to let others know it? **Stop it!**

Psalms 140:4-5   Psalms 10:2-4

Note the key points of each verse below:

_____

_____

_____

_____

Are you so filled with pride that you cannot see when you are doing wrong and hurting others? **Stop it!** The Bible describes the selfish people as ones who are full of pride and violence, and they look for profits without regard for anything. Selfish people also make fun of other people and speak evil of others. Are you too high minded to befriend someone? Do you think they are low class, and unworthy of your friendship? **Stop it!** The Bible describes people with this trait, as selfish and hating good doctrine.

Isolating yourself from people for a short while, in order to commune with God (Yahuah) directly and recharge, is not a bad thing. In fact, it is good for you to give God (Yahuah) that time. Jesus(Yahusha) would often withdraw from the crowd for short periods in order to commune with His father, Yahweh(Yahuah), God.

Dealing with people daily takes enormous amounts of spiritual, emotional and sometimes physical energy, so take the time to get away but for a short while. Do not live in isolation from others and never from God(Yahuah). Be friendly and show love toward others to rid yourself of selfishness.

Be loving and remove selfishness and take a step toward Freedom from the CURSE.

LICENTIOUSNESS

Do you defile your holy temple body with sexual immorality? This attitude is helping to dig your own grave, and is keeping

163

you under the CURSE of poverty. **Stop it!** Before long all your good character will be squandered, and you will be CURSED if you don't change.

Ellen White (Testimonies on Sexual Behaviour, Adultery and Divorce, 1989) writes,

At Baal-peor. The crime that brought the judgments of God upon Israel was that of licentiousness. The forwardness of women to entrap souls did not end at Baal-peor... Satan was most active in seeking to make Israel's overthrow complete. Balak by the advice of Balaam laid the snare. Israel would have bravely met their enemies in battle, and resisted them, and come off conquerors; but when women invited their attention and sought their company and beguiled them by their charms, they did not resist temptations... Those who had never flinched in battle, who were brave men, did not barricade their souls to resist temptation to indulge their basest passions.

This is part of the problem we face today as individuals, as groups, and as communities. The systematic plan for the sexualization of our youth, has led to the strengthening of their baser human desires without the development of self control. What we are seeing manifested today is the result of this plan being implemented 40, 50, or more years ago.

Our young people are being hurt in their formative years when character and personality is being hardened. This injury impacts their entire life. How many teenage girls are forced into sexual relations when they were not ready? How many teenage boys felt peer pressure by other boys to dabble in sexual relations though they were not ready? We're currently living in the fruit of decades of subtle sexual influences on our young people who have grown up to become adults who regard sexuality lightly. People call it rape culture but it is really a hypersexualized culture without self-control.

Proverbs 6:28-29   Proverbs 6:32-33
Malachi 3:5   Matthew 5:27-28

Note the key points of each verse below:

_____

_____

_____

_____

_____

Immodesty is now the norm and men and women have thrown off modesty and comeliness. You need to choose for yourself to embrace modesty and comeliness again. It starts in your mind.

Let's not forget the immorality that stems from alcohol consumption. People tend to lose their inhibitions when they drink alcohol which leads to sexual immorality, brawling/fighting, cursing, blasphemy, and more.

Leviticus 10:9	Deuteronomy 29:6	Jeremiah 35
1 Samuel 1:14-15	1 Samuel 25:36-37	Isaiah 5:11
Proverbs 4:14-17	Proverbs 23:29-34	Isaiah 5:22
Jeremiah 51:7	Daniel 1:8	Joel 1:5
Romans 14:21	Titus 1:7	Titus 2:3

Note the key points of each verse below:

_____

_____

_____

_____

_____

In Deuteronomy 29:6, it states, "Ye have not eaten bread, neither have ye drunk wine or strong drink: that ye might know that I am the LORD your God." This was referring to the 40 years of wondering in the wilderness. It is interesting to note that the people Moses brought out of the Egypt are referred to here as being sober, that is, not drinking any alcoholic beverages for 40 years. Can you make the decision to give up alcohol now and not touch it again for 40 years? It seems like a difficult challenge for a culture that so highly regards the consumption of alcohol. Alcohol impairs good judgement and facilitates a licentious lifestyle. If you are seeking a holy lifestyle, peace of mind, more connection with the spiritual kingdom of heaven, then alcohol is your enemy. Exercise sexual self-control and take a step toward Freedom from the CURSE.

LEARN to DO RIGHT

How is it possible to learn to do right? We learn to walk as a baby. Have you ever looked at the behaviour of little babies? Looking at my baby brother, when he was old enough to navigate things to his mouth, he tried to put all kinds of stuff in his mouth. His stuffed toys, his finger, his pacifier were all game. When we see babies putting bad stuff in their mouths, we tell them no, and correct them. By doing this, babies are learning to do right, because their natural instinct was to do the wrong thing.

In much the same way, we have to train ourselves to do right. When you were a child, I'm sure your parent didn't teach you "buy low, sell high." My parents never did. As an adult, I had to attempt to train myself by reading books, talking to people, praying and seeking information from my trusted advisors, mentors, family, and many other friends and colleagues.

1 Samuel 12:22-24   Proverbs 4:1-2
Titus 2:7-12   1 Corinthians 13:11

Note the key points of each verse below:

_____

_____

_____

_____

_____

The prophet Samuel in 1 Samuel 12, relates to us that God (Yahuah) will not reject us, (His people) as he wants to make us His people. However, we are to continuously pray for each other, teach others the right ways we know, and serve our God (Yahuah) with a reverent and faithful heart.

Does this verse from Samuel mean anything to you? Think about it. It seems here that we are being given a directive. We are being shown what we should do. So you say, "What do I do?" Your task, find a teacher and learn as much as you can. Your teacher doesn't have to be a university educated triple PhD person. Academics rarely have the answer to spiritual matters, but some do.

Find a genuine, sincere person who has demonstrated that he or she is a citizen of heaven. Find someone who has been a good steward of what has been entrusted to him or her. I'd love to talk with you, but it would be difficult for me to talk to the multitude of people who will read this book. So how can you spend time with me? Read this book, take the 30-day challenge, or enrol in the online course. I've poured my God given creative inspiration into these resource just for you. So you can spend time with me that way. This book is already a good start. I've written this with the hope that you will learn.

I have also created an online and updated version of my Break The Poverty Curse course. With the course, you get to study with me as I walk you through the precepts and principles from the Bible. The course link and description is available after the final chapter of this book.

The Bible also instructs us not to repay evil with evil, but let goodness follow us all the days of our lives. If you want to learn to do right, I recommend:

1. Spend time daily reading the Bible and Bible commentaries from qualified sources.
2. Find other people who demonstrate the true love of God(Yahuah) for their fellow man, in public and in private. Learn only what is good from them.
3. Memorize and follow the Ten Commandments in Exodus 20 and the two given by Jesus(Yahusha). Seek God directly for his guidance in helping you do right.

Read and understand the guidelines given by Yahuah. The Bible says that God came down from Heaven to Mount Sinai and spoke with the Israelites, and taught them right ordinances, true laws, good statutes and commandments.

Learn to do right and take a step toward Freedom from the CURSE.

SEEK Justice

Justice seems to be a scarce commodity in these times, but you are to seek it, and reflect it in your daily life.

Genesis 18:19   2 Samuel 8:15
Titus 2:7-9   1 Kings 10:9
Psalm 82:2-5   Proverbs 8:14-15

Note the key points of each verse below:

_____

_____

_____

_____

_____

- Do not spread false reports. Do not help a wicked man by being a malicious witness.
- Do not follow the crowd in doing wrong. Mob mentality is not acceptable.
- If you come across your enemy's lost or damaged possession, be sure to return it to him. Treat his possession as though it were your own.
- Do not deny justice to poor people in their lawsuits.
- Have nothing to do with false charges, and do not condemn an innocent/honest person. (In words or deeds)
- Do not accept bribes or gifts or self-serving riders on government bills to be approved by parliament, because it obscures right and perverts righteousness.
- Do not oppress others.

God (Yahuah) understood groupthink long before psychologists even had a clue. Thousands of years ago he understood that people were prone to follow the crowd. He told us not to. Do not go along with a lying crowd. You simply need to remain truthful. Live with truthfulness in your life and it can help you crowd out the wicked impulses.

There's a video clip I saw on social media. An Australian radio show host called a stranger on the show and pretended to be a guy going in for a job interview. He told the guy he was going to use him as a reference. The guy, I'll call Jim told him no problem. Then the show called Jim live on-air and began to ask Jim about the host who pretended to be someone else. Listeners could hear Jim giving the host a glowing reference. He was a good man. He did volunteer work. He saved the company lots of money, and on and on. Finally the radio show host couldn't contain himself and burst into the call and said Jim is the best bloke(guy) in the world. Jim, a complete stranger was lying as a reference for someone who was being interviewed for a job and who he did not know. The video was very popular on social media.

I have a huge problem with this scene. I would never call Jim the best guy in the world. He's lying for a complete stranger when he is supposed to be a character reference. A reference is a judge of a person's character and ethics. So Jim can't possibly know the character of a person who he does not know. But I know Jim's character is a liar. Though he is using his lies for the appearance of a good deed.

What if that was a real situation and the person being interviewed was a scoundrel and thief? Jim's glowing reference of character and ethics might have gotten the person the job and endangered the company.

The end does not justify the means. Jim lied to help a fake stranger get a fake job but Jim should not be applauded for this.

Jim's heart might have been in the right place but he used dishonest means to achieve the objectives. Cheating in professional sports gets athletes disqualified precisely because the end goal of winning does not justify the means of cheating to win.

Here's a different example. In 2016 USA Senator Elizabeth Warren was questioning a bank CEO about a scandal involving defrauding bank customers of millions of dollars. Warren asked the CEO if he had resigned because of the rampant corruption under his policies? He said no. She asked if he returned any of the bonuses and salary he received for running the bank during this scheme. He said no. She asked if he fired any senior executives involved in the oversight during this scandal. He said no. She blatantly told him that he should be investigated and criminally charged for his policies resulting in this scheme. He profited via the increased value of his shares in the bank plus his bonuses and perks.

She told him that if a teller took a stack of $20s and put it in their pocket, they would probably be looking at jail time but he made millions off this scheme and he thinks he will just be able to walk away.

Here is an example of a woman standing up for true justice. She is standing up for the poor $12/hr worker who was forced to be part of this fraud scheme out of fear of being fired for not making quotas. And at the same time, she was telling the big man at the top that he was not exempt from his personal accountability in this matter.

Now in this situation we can see Elizabeth Warren demonstrate a quality of seeking justice.

Justice in the tiny things are just as important as justice in the bigger things of life. Seek and practise justice and take a step toward Freedom from the CURSE.

RELIEVE the oppressed

Relieve the oppressed, you say. Where are these oppressed? Maybe you live in a developed country where people are free. Maybe there is no war, no political instability, no civil unrest or anything that seems oppressive to you?

Judges 2:18	1 Samuel 12:3-4	Job 20:19-29
Psalms 9:9	Ecclesiastes 4:1	Psalms 10:18
Acts 10:38		

Note the key points of each verse below:

_____

_____

_____

171

_____

_____

_____

_____

_____

Look again. See the church member treated badly by religious zealots and legalists. See the poor person begging for change for food on the street. See the housewife who wears the bruises of an emotionally and physically abusive relationship. See the teenage girl whose life has been shattered by sexual abuse. See the young child too shy or too ashamed to talk about the poverty at home.

See the person looking back at you in the mirror. Look deep.

Oppression is not only from man, but from the evil one, the devil. In Acts 10 we see that Messiah, Jesus(Yahusha) was given power of the Holy Spirit to heal all who were oppressed of the devil. Spiritual oppression is many times more burdensome than man's oppression. We must also relieve this form of oppression, where God (Yahuah) has enabled us.

Oppression takes many forms in our time. There is nothing to stop you from being an angel of compassion to another person in need. The King of Heaven Himself will be a refuge to the oppressed, so when you do this work, you align yourself with Him and flee the impact of the CURSE.

If our God, Yahweh(Yahuah), will personally take up the cause of the poor to uplift them, then what will be the outcome of the person who fights against Him by oppressing the poor? It is better to be on Yahuah's side, by helping to relieve the suffering of the poor. By the way, we're poor also until God(Yahuah) changes our status.

Relieve the oppressed and take a step toward Freedom from the CURSE.

CORRECT the oppressor

This is a hard thing for any normal person to do. There is no doubt that it is far more difficult when you are coming from a position of complete powerlessness.

Psalms 72:4-5   Proverbs 3:31-33   Job 15:20-22
Proverbs 28:16   Zechariah 9:8-9

Note the key points of each verse below:

_____

_____

_____

_____

_____

_____

_____

However this brings to mind a previous boss. She told me that her principle was to stand up for a waitress, cashier or customer service person being insulted or abused by another customer. She said that usually, an employee couldn't stick up for himself or herself, for fear of losing the job, but as a customer, she could tell the other customer that their behaviour was unacceptable. In her own way, she was standing up to the oppressor. Maybe she didn't establish world peace by her actions, but her actions certainly meant the world to the employee being oppressed. I really admired that about Linda.

There is a popular saying that goes, "The wicked prosper when the righteous do nothing." I'd go on to say the oppressor prospers when no one speaks up.

The Bible verses in this section give a stern warning about what will happen to the oppressor. Even if you only showed them these verses, it is correcting them. In Zechariah we see that no oppressor can touch one who Christ(Yahusha) protects, so speak up boldly when God(Yahuah) gives you the words.

We have ways to make our voices heard even if we are too weak to speak ourselves. We could join the union, tell the law/police, seek a lawyer or write a letter to the newspaper, join an association, NGO, activist group, or just do something. Doing nothing is not an option. In 2016 in Toronto, a group of Black activists occupied the space in front of the police headquarters in Toronto for two weeks. It was early spring so the weather was still cold. There was some freezing rain. There was light snow. The weather was less than ideal for Spring. Yet, those protesters remained there for the two weeks. Finally the Ontario premier agreed to meet with leaders to discuss the terrible unjust killings of young black persons.

The group felt that people of the black race were being oppressed. The protesters wanted answers and those guilty of dishonourable behaviour to be held accountable.

Correct the oppressor and take a step toward Freedom from the CURSE.

DEFEND the fatherless (orphan) and PLEAD for the widow

These two go hand in hand. I remember the movie 'Scent of a Woman', starring Al Pacino. The main character was a blind retired soldier who happen to be in the care of this young man for the weekend. Over the course of the weekend, they become friends and the retired soldier finds out that the boy may be in trouble with his school, because he was a witness to something. A hearing was to be convened on the following Monday. The soldier asked the boy if his father would be there at his side. The boy replied that his father was dead and his stepfather was a jerk. So his parents were not going to be there to speak up for him. Al Pacino's character went to the school on behalf of the parents, and spoke in the boy's defense. This for me represents a prime example of one person defending the orphan. The character was not a literal orphan but a symbolic orphan.

Exodus 22:22-24	Deuteronomy 10:16-19
Deuteronomy 27:19	Deuteronomy 14:27-29
Psalms 10:12-15	Deuteronomy 24:19-22
Psalms 82:1-6	Isaiah 1:16-18

Note the key points of each verse below:

_____

_____

_____

_____

_____

_____

_____

How can this possibly apply to you? You need to get to know the young people around you. Sometimes you have to stick up for someone who is young, or provide guidance to a youth in need. Who knows if the very moment you enter someone's life, when everything seemed so desperate, you could help that person embrace a turning point. At that moment, he or she may feel that there is no father or mother or brother or sister or anyone who can help, but the Almighty Yahuah has placed you in that life, to give that person a second chance. Defend him/her emotionally, physically, financially or any way within your means.

Defend the fatherless and the widows and take a step toward Freedom from the CURSE.

Be WILLING and OBEDIENT

To be willing and obedient, the onus lies with you. For anyone willing to work, there is work. For anyone willing to learn, there are people, books and courses and institutions. For anyone willing to obey, there is mercy.

Proverbs 25:12	Isaiah 1:19
Isaiah 42:24	Deuteronomy 28:1-14
Acts 6:7	2 Corinthians 2:8-11
Jeremiah 7:23	Deuteronomy 11:26-28
Psalm 37:3-4	

Note the key points of each verse below:

_____

_____

_____

_____

_____

In Deuteronomy 28: Yahuah has a wealth of blessings for those who obey Him. What is a blessing? A blessing in the spiritual context of our discussion, is something that promotes or contributes to happiness, well-being and prosperity. But the spiritual blessings of Yahuah manifest themselves in the natural world, because His power brought the world into being.

Some of the blessings which accrue to the obedient person include:

- Being blessed in the city and in the country: Whether you live in the city or you live in the country, or wherever you find yourself living, the environment will be one that is beneficial to you.
- Having the fruit of your womb blessed: You will not have to wonder if you'll have any children to carry on your name. Husbands and wives will never have to fear infertility.
- Having victory over your enemies: You will not be the downtrodden, misused and abused person. God has promised to stand up for you and will give you the victory over your enemies.
- Having all your works blessed: Whether you are a painter, plumber, account manager, director or whatever position, you can take heart that whatever you put your hand to do will be a success.
- Being blessed with so much you never need to borrow: You will have so much excess, that you can give freely to the needy. You will lend to others or simply give away because you have such abundance.

Isn't that a great feeling? Think of being the person people come to when they need something done right.

Think of being assured that you will not be a failure, and your efforts will not be in vain or wasted. It can happen but it takes willingness and obedience. And here's a little known bonus, people who align themselves with a person who is living in the blessing, can also share in some blessings, as long as they are not evil and attracting the CURSE.

In Psalm 37 we are encouraged to "Enjoy serving the Lord and He will give you what you want." When we exercise obedience and submit to God's plans, we can have trust and confidence in our desires. Remember God (Yahuah) is too gracious and loving to ask you to do something that is not good for you.

Have a willing and obedient attitude and take a step toward Freedom from the CURSE.

Your Choice

I encourage you at once to begin to set your affairs in order for whatever value you place on life. Let us summarize all that we have learnt in this chapter. We know that there are cosmic rules in place within the universe which govern certain actions. One action creates a reaction in direct response to the rule.

The creator of the universe is just, and each person will get the reward he or she deserves.

If one deserves a CURSE, then it will come upon him, and likewise, if he deserves a BLESSING, it too will come upon him. However, the key is that we hold the swaying vote.

We can choose the CURSE by our actions or we can choose the BLESSINGS instead. God (Yahuah) wants us all to be winners and to prove to the world that His ways are right by our example.

With this knowledge firmly taking hold on your mind, you can begin to renew your thinking so that you have a mind like the mind of Christ(Yahusha) in you. Renew your mind with the goodness you are learning in this book.

* * *

Course Note: Write the key points from the course material for this section below.

_____

_____

_____

_____

_____

_____

_____

_____

_____

_____

_____

Is it important to make the decision to change.

* * *

Stop And Think

Don't just rush into the next chapter. Examine your emotions. Why do you feel this way? Can you really become free from the CURSE?

Realization: Now I understand truly how much bigger than myself this problem is. I could no more change it, than I can change the direction of gravity. I know that the Creator of the universe is on my side and His power is sufficient to get me out from under the CURSE. I have taken the steps in this chapter to move forward out of the curse.

Prayer: Almighty Yauhah, I now understand why I was under the CURSE. Please forgive me for my sins and wilful disobedience of your laws. Teach me of you and your ways. Help me to follow you wholeheartedly. Renew my heart, my mind, my body and soul for you. Break this CURSE for your name sake. Thank you for loving me enough to intervene in my life at this present time. Please fill my life with your love and help me share all you teach me with others around me. Blessed be Yahuah, God Almighty. Amen.

Affirmation: Today I know the truth and I AM FREE.

* * *

Go to checkpoint #6:
www.breakthepovertycurse.com

Write Your Personal Insights Here

_____

_____

_____

_____

_____

_____

_____

_____

_____

_____

* * * * *

In our course on Breaking the Poverty Curse at Berkeley Academy, we tackle the topic in more details and give you more fast start money ideas for your cash flow situation. You are simply lacking in some core aspects of fast cash seeding and reaping. Check out the course at http://berkeley.academy/our-courses/

* * * * *

The Physical Dimension

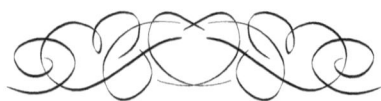

III

The Trap Of Life

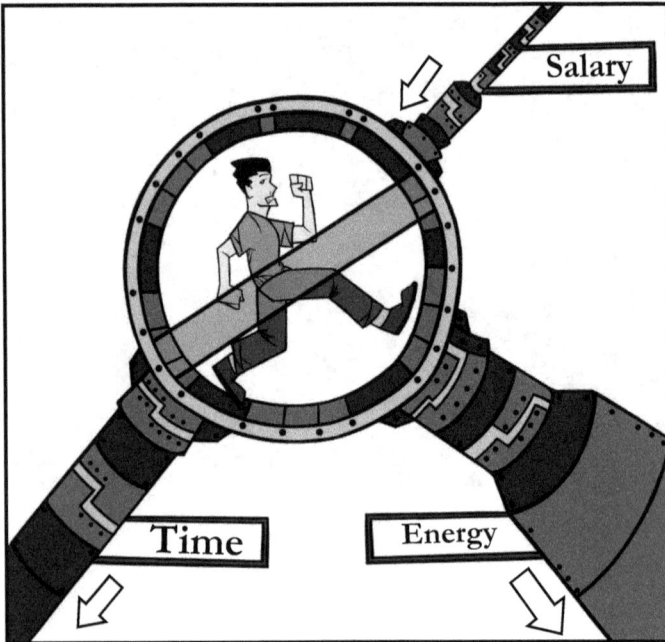

In this Physical Dimension section of the book, we're going to learn principles that can help us structure our lives to avoid the Trap of Life.

Raising Your Shields (Defence)

Chapter 7

* * *

The law of the LORD is perfect, converting the soul: the testimony of the LORD is sure, making wise the simple. The statutes of the LORD are right, rejoicing the heart: the commandment of the LORD is pure, enlightening the eyes. - Psalms 19:7-8

Crime is contagious. If the government becomes a lawbreaker, it breeds contempt for the law. - US Supreme Court Justice Louis Brandeis (1928)

When your actions are mindful, lawful, and loving, you will be loved by people around you plus heaven will appreciate your impact on earth. ~ Vaughn Berkeley, MBA

* * *

The first six chapters of this book have been about the spiritual and mental warfare in the battle against this CURSE of Poverty. In section I, we looked at what was poverty. We also considered the spiritual reasons and their temporal manifestations, which can either be a contributing factor, symptom or the result of the CURSE of poverty. This problem is so heinous that it is like a multi-headed hydra.

Section II led you through the mental aspects of the POVERTY CURSE condition. You also discovered the path to healing the CURSE of poverty from a spiritual and mental standpoint. This is especially important, because the battle is first won on the spiritual plain and mental plain, and then manifested on the physical/temporal one. Sections I & II introduced you to the brand new car to take you on the journey. This section is the key you need to start that beautiful car.

There are some fundamental learning points you need to know in order to help you contextualize the information given previously.

Heaven is the centre of a Kingdom. God (Yahuah) is the king of this kingdom whose capital is called Heaven. All earthly kingdoms have rules or laws, don't they? Yes.

Every government whether monarchy or democracy or otherwise, has laws in place which regulate the activity of people. The kingdom of God (Yahuah) has rules since its creation and long before the earth was created. It is written that war broke out in heaven, the capital of the kingdom, and Lucifer (Satan) was cast out to the earth.

These rules are eternal and cannot be disregarded because they are the foundation of an eternal kingdom.

What shall I do to INHERIT ETERNITY? And he said unto him, Why callest thou me good? there is none good but one, that is, God: but if thou wilt enter into life, keep the commandments.
~ Matthew 19:17

breakthepovertycurse.com

The Ten Commandments

These great commandments were written in stone by the finger of God (Yahweh) and given to mankind via His ambassador, Moses, at that time. Thus it is paramount that you fully know them and live them daily.

Exodus 20:2-17 Deuteronomy 5:6-21

1. I am the LORD thy God, which have brought thee out of the land of Egypt, out of the house of bondage. Thou shalt have no other gods before me. (Exodus 20:1-3)

God (Yahuah) is telling us here that we should have no other gods. He is one and only.

For example, other gods can also be your stomach if you worship food, or money if your actions show you worship it. They can be people if you idolize them and worship them. They can also be the various gods of various cultures. The creator, Yahweh, is our true God because He brought us out from the slavery(bondage) of the CURSE.

Egypt is symbolic in our time. For us today, it represents a place/time in our lives where we faced religious oppression, and perhaps had our freedoms limited through the CURSE. God (Yahuah) has brought us out of that. He wants you free today. That's why you're reading this book.

An important note here is that we are all in bondage to sin on the earth until Jesus(Yahusha), messiah, sets us free. Remember Jesus(Yahusha) healed a woman who had been sick 18 years on a Sabbath day.

When there was contention among the religious leaders, Jesus(Yahusha) told then, "Ought not this woman, a daughter of Abraham, whom Satan bound for eighteen years, be loosed from this bond on this Sabbath day?" (Luke 13:16. KJV)

Our God (Yahuah) is the God who sets us free and brings us out of the house of bondage of Satan.

Our purpose therefore is to seek God with all our heart, mind, and soul.

2. Thou shalt not make unto thee any graven image, or any likeness of any thing that is in heaven above, or that is in the earth beneath, or that is in the water under the earth. Thou shalt not bow down thyself to them, nor serve them: for I the LORD thy God am a jealous God, visiting the iniquity of the fathers upon the children unto the third and fourth generation of them that hate me; And shewing mercy unto thousands of them that love me, and keep my commandments. (Exodus 20:4-6)

We are being commanded here to not set up or bow down to anything made by humans, for assistance in the act of worship. Idols can be statues set up in temples or even the cross of Christ has become an idol.

People believe there is power in the cross, they wear them on their bodies or tattoo them on their skin. Taking anything made by God or man-made and attributing some supernatural power to that is idolatry. It has severe consequences. Here there is a reminder of the multi-generational CURSE. To be free from the CURSE, never worship anything made with human hands or any created thing in the heavens, or the earth, or beneath the earth.

God (Yahuah) made man in his own image. Humans then, being made in the image of God, must carry themselves with a regal dignity befitting the form they were created within. It is an affront to God (Yahuah) to lower that image of man to anything beneath God.

For example, when we say that humans are equal to animals or call humans animals, we devalue humans in order to elevate animals, thus making the animals an idol. When we attribute some supernatural power to statues made of wood, stone, clay, or anything, and we elevate those things to a status on par with God, we devalue ourselves and negate the great gift bestowed upon humanity at creation, that is, to be made in the image of the King of all creation.

3.Thou shalt not take the name of the LORD thy God in vain; for the LORD will not hold him guiltless that taketh his name in vain. (Exodus 20:7)

God (Yahuah) is a king of a vast kingdom. There are times when people use the name of Jesus(Yahusha) as a profane word, or shout "oh my God", without even thinking of God (Yahuah). This is taking His name in vain. There are also Christians and/or people who claim to be followers of God, Yahweh(Yahuah), but their actions and practises go against God (Yahuah). They continually take His name in vain. If we say we are Christians or followers of Yahuah, then our thoughts, words and deeds should reflect this claim. God(Yahuah) wants us to show mercy, compassion, forgiveness, kindness, and love to others in truth. He wants us to stand up for truth, and righteousness. Those who deny those things and call themselves Christians are taking God's name in vain.

4.Remember the Sabbath day, to keep it holy. Six days shalt thou labour, and do all thy work: But the seventh day is the Sabbath of the LORD thy God: in it thou shalt not do any work, thou, nor thy son, nor thy daughter, thy manservant, nor thy maidservant, nor thy cattle, nor thy stranger that is within thy gates: For in six days the LORD made

heaven and earth, the sea, and all that in them is, and rested the seventh day: wherefore the LORD blessed the Sabbath day, and hallowed it. (Exodus 20:8-11)

The seventh day is called Saturday. This command directs us to rest from our regular work on Saturday. How can we know this? The Jewish people have been meticulous in keeping the Sabbath since it was taught to them by God(Yahuah), and written by Moses. If we partake of this rest, we get a special blessing, which rejuvenates us for more productive work the following week.

We also acknowledge God, Yahweh(Yahuah) supremacy by resting on His Holy day. In the entire Bible, God (Yahuah) never changed Sabbath to Sunday. Even Jesus(Yahusha) who is the role model for the believer never worshipped on any other day besides Saturday (Sabbath).

A series of articles which ran in the Baltimore Catholic Mirror in Fall of 1893 later compiled in the booklet, Rome's Challenge, notes:

> "Protestants' claim, that they stand upon the written word [Holy Bible] only, it is not true. Their profession of holding the Scripture alone as the standard of faith, is false. PROOF: The written word explicitly enjoins the observance of the seventh day as the Sabbath...Yet they not only reject the observance of the Sabbath enjoined in the written word, but they have adopted and do practise the observance of Sunday, for which they have only the tradition of the [Catholic] Church." [emphasis added]

Unfortunately many sincere Christians believe they are worshipping God, Yahweh(Yahuah) on Sunday, and so they do all their shopping and other work on Sabbath (Saturday), thereby profaning His Holy Sabbath. The Roman Catholic Church is the sole owner of Sunday worship, and Protestants who claim the Bible as their only authority yet worship on

Sunday, are sadly incongruous. This opens up access to the
Poverty CURSE.

What should be done on Sabbath (Saturday) is, rest from our
weekly labour, do good works in the community and
worship God (Yahuah). Remember, Jesus(Yahusha) said it is
lawful to do good on Sabbath. Try it for yourself. Keep the
Sabbath (Saturday) holy for a 7, 12, or 21 weeks and see
what blessings come your way. Rest from your weekly work
on that day. Do good work in your community. Bond with
your family. Try it.

5.Honour thy father and thy mother: that thy days may be long upon the land which the LORD thy God giveth thee. (Exodus 20:12)

I've noticed that some children in North America do not
have that love for their parents. Years ago, I knew of one
wealthy lawyer whose father had a stroke, and who was
being cared for by his mother, who worked part-time in a
lowly job. The lawyer had many cars and much real estate,
but his parents lived in abject poverty. Thus, he has opened
the way for the CURSE on himself and his children. Also,
his children are learning the way he treated their
grandparents, and will surely learn to treat him the same way,
when he gets old. This rule reminds us to look after our
parents the best that we can as they get older, because they
deserve that from us regardless of the past.

God (Yahuah) loves parents who take their duty seriously.
The parent starts out like a god to the infant. The survival of
the infant depends 100% on the parents. They cloth the
infant, they feed the infant, they change the pee and poop.
They teach the infant language skills and as the infant grows
into a young child more things are taught to the child and
more nurturing takes place until the child is an adult.
I truly believe that a person cannot fully appreciate the
power of God(Yahuah) and the responsibility God (Yahuah)
takes in our lives unless that person becomes a parent or

guardian of a baby or child. I personally have learnt so much about God's(Yahuah) relationship to me in the ordinary everyday act of being a father to my children.

When parents fail their children, those kids can grow up to become broken adults on the inside even though they may look perfectly fine outwardly. Nevertheless, God (Yahuah) is able to heal all fractures within our soul, and heart because He is our creator.

And when the love of God(Yahuah) dwells in your heart, you still try to honour your parents even though they were wicked to you, because you seek to honour God. Honouring them does not mean condoning their wickedness or enabling their wickedness. It simply means if they are hungry feed them, if they are lonely, call them, if they are depressed, cheer them up. If they are poor and you are rich, lift them up out of poverty. Being a parent is a life-long duty. Even if they were terrible parents and still are, we cannot discard them in their old age.

In God's (Yahuah) love for parents, He expects children to show them honour and respect. Remember, it also contains a promise of long life.

6. Thou shalt not kill. (Exodus 20:13)

This command is simple. Do not physically or mentally kill anyone. The Bible also teaches that whoever hates another is a murderer. Hatred of your fellow man breaks this rule, even if you never openly act on it. To follow this rule you must nurture love and forgiveness for your brethren in the faith and by extension, those who have not accepted truth and righteousness.

Killing entails loss and pain and suffering. Think about your pet dog or cat which you love. If that animal got hit by a car so that it died, you would be grieving for the loss of your beloved pet. A few years back I read a newspaper story about a police officer shooting an animal at night and killing it. He ran it over with his car first. He thought the animal was a wild coyote. Turns out the animal was a very elderly dog that was partially blind and partially deaf. It had wondered out of the yard and ended up in the tragic affair. The owners of that dog grieved for their beloved animal. It made the news, remember. There's a youtube video on it somewhere.

There are billions of animals killed/slaughtered each year just so humans can indulge in meat. These animals are loved. They are mothers and children. Their lives are filled with suffering and misery caused by humans who are paid in order to provide their flesh to people to eat it. To consume the flesh of animals is to endorse senseless, inhumane, and unnecessary killing.

When the kingdom of heaven is restored on earth, all living creatures will be plant-based. Search the scriptures for yourself and see it says the lion will eat grass like the ox. No killing and no death will be part of the kingdom.

Every living creature will be plant-based (flesh-free) when the kingdom of heaven is restored on earth. If that is the case, a believer cannot and should not reject veganism now on earth. Give up flesh now in order to prepare your mindset for heaven.

Thus, you should not endorse killing now on earth or foster hatred in your heart toward your fellow humans.

7. Thou shalt not commit adultery. (Exodus 20:14)

This command is simple. Do not physically or mentally engage in sexual relations with another, who is not your spouse. With the prevalence of internet porn, sexuality in advertising of everything, immodest dress of men and women, the temptation to fantasize about another or engage in an extra marital relation is present. With modern day smartphones and apps that allow users to send messages that are secure and are destroyed immediately upon reading, people take that as more liberty to disregard this command. There are even men or women who take pleasure in being the "side-*ick." They do not respect the marriage relationship sanctified by God(Yahuah).

If a married man or woman approaches you for an extra marital relationship, you have the choice to tell them no. Just say no. If they ask you 100 times, just say no 100 times. Like the song says, "My name is NO. My number is NO. My sign is NO. You better let it go."

What about a divorced person? Jesus(Yahusha) gave very clear instructions that no divorce is valid unless it was on the grounds of fornication. And whoever marries a divorced person commits adultery and is living in adultery with that person. Divorcing for any reason so that you can enter in an intimate relationship with another side-*ick, is adultery. Marrying a divorced person is adultery.

Matthew 5:32   Matthew 19:9
Galations 5:19-21

Note the key points of each verse below:

_____

_____

_____

_____

_____

_____

_____

If a person has intercourse with a married person, it is adultery. When Jesus(Yahusha) expanded the truth of the matter, he showed no divorce is legal unless it is for fornication. An invalid reason for divorce in heaven invalidates the divorce. If a person has intercourse with a "divorced" person it is the act of adultery. The act occurs one time for one act.

However when someone decides to marry a "divorced" person then the adultery is committed anew day after day, month after month, year after year, for as long as the two people remain in the adulterous union. This is because their "marriage" is not legal in heaven. There was to be no remarriage after a divorce. Jesus(Yahusha) told us plainly, anyone who marries a divorced person commits adultery.

Story time: I've encountered many relationships over the years and with social media platforms, it's easy to find examples of things which should not be. I've seen a guy who divorced his first wife, made her life hell through the process, then go on to marry a second woman. After living years with this woman, he divorced her and made her life hell during the divorce. And to show his reprobate mind and sinful nature, he was openly dating and putting pictures of his new girlfriend up on social media while still in the midst of the divorce from wife number 2. What's worst is that this reprobate man calls himself a Christian. His second marriage was an adulterous relationship and now he is about to ruin another woman's life in a sinful relationship.

Galations 5:19-21 shows that that there is a group of people who will not inherit the kingdom of God. These include adulterers.

Remarriage after divorce is living in adultery if your ex-spouse is still alive. Marriage began in the garden of Eden before sin and the fall of mankind. It was thus meant to be an eternal institution. Sin brought death into the world and death is the only thing that severs a marriage bond on earth. Even if you are unhappy with your husband or wife, you are honour bound and duty bound to find a path to reconciliation. Ask God(Yahuah) to work it out. He can change their heart or stop their heart if they love wickedness.

Story time: I know of a man who married a woman while they were young. He divorced his faithful wife a few years later but made her life hell throughout the divorce process. His wife was broken but not shattered. He went on to marry another woman. The faithful ex-wife had adulterous liaisons with men and ended up becoming pregnant a few times. The wicked man and his new wife lived a rough life yet he was still in the church. His ex-spouse who was a faithful woman in her youth now had a string of bad relationships, adulterous liasons, and was left to raise children on her own. She eventually married a man who loved her and God(Yahuah) and this woman and new husband lived a hard life. Now both "married" couples are living a lifestyle of adultery. And the fruit of the previous adulterous liaisons are an ongoing part of their lives and struggle.

The Poverty CURSE is the loophole that Satan will now attempt to have placed upon each couple because of their lifestyle. Satan is like a roaring lion seeking whom he might devour and by any means necessary including using the universal laws that govern the Poverty CURSE against God's (Yahuah) fallen children.

These kinds of adulterous relations are so commonplace in society today even as it was in the days when Jesus(Yahusha) walked the earth. In fact, these "marriages" have become acceptable in modern society. People do not want to hear or be told that their current marriage is an adulterous one. It offends them and they will tell you off, get angry with you, or call you nasty stuff. They may call you a hater, a legalist, a person who wants to break up "marriages" or some other hurtful thing. Yet, adultery is an offensive odour to heaven because it is not what God (Yahuah) wants in the lives of His children. Yet, because people are hard hearted on this issue, they rather live in second, third, or fourth marriages. All these are living in adultery. No adulterer will enter the kingdom of heaven. By telling adulterers this in order to get them a ticket to heaven, they see you as the bad person. Shame on those who love wickedness so that they reject the light and call good evil and evil good.

So you ask, "Vaughn, why don't pastors, or church or temple leaders preach this message?" The answer is really simple. These "religious leaders" love man more than they love God (Yahuah). It is because to preach this heavenly standard as it pertains to marriage is very unpopular. Congregations may decide to cut their tithes, offerings, and donations which is less money for the church leaders. Another reason is that some of those same church pastors, elders, rabbi, or other "religious leader" are themselves living in an adulterous "marriage." Thus to speak against it is to condemn themselves and they would refuse to do that and expose their sinfulness to the congregations. And so they make null and void the word of God (Yahuah) through their unfaithful preaching of the scripture.

These scriptures help us see the truth in the matter.

Proverbs 6:32   Jeremiah 29:23
James 2:11   2 Peter 2:14

Note the key points of each verse below:

_____

_____

_____

_____

_____

_____

_____

This makes you gasp, right? It makes me gasp too and almost ask the question, "if that's the case, then how can anyone be saved?" Thank God (Yahuah) that Jesus (Yahusha) provided the answer when his disciples asked him the same question. Jesus (Yahuah) said, "With man, it is impossible, but with God, all things are possible."

God (Yahuah) may be able to save his lost children living in this sinful relationship and to take them out of the sinful relationship. But look at the fruit that comes from the seed of divorce and subsequent living a life in adultery. Couples have their hearts weekly pierced through with many sorrows. God(Yahuah) knows the sorrows that can arise from adulterous relationships and so He is in wisdom and love, gave us the command against it, in order to save us from the heartache and pain.

A quick note here on those who preach the scriptures. Any person claiming to preach the gospel truth of God(Yahuah) while living in a "marriage" of adultery, is disqualified from preaching the word of God. Why? They have wilfully denied the scriptures on this matter, and will twist the scriptures to support their lifestyle and truth will be mingled with error. Thus they will lead others in the body of believers astray in order to justify themselves.

They must end the "marriage" of adultery and then dedicate themselves to serving God (Yahuah) and preaching the gospel. In this manner, it requires them to make a sacrifice. And I know this is a difficult thing to say and to do. With emotions involved your "wife" or "husband" feels like a part of your own body. Yet, Jesus said, if one of your members offend you, remove it as it is better to go into heaven lame than be whole for the destruction of hell.

It's really a tough call. But ultimately it comes down to whether you love your "new marriage spouse" more than you love God (Yahuah). The scripture cannot be broken and Jesus(Yahusha) himself told us that anyone who marries a divorced person commits adultery. And both the man and the woman are guilty of adultery not just the "new spouse."

A divorced person is off limits to intimate relations and to remarriage, period.

Can you ask God (Yahuah) to forgive you for your adultery today while you are sleeping in the same adultery bed every night? Can you have intercourse with your man or woman tomorrow after you prayed for forgiveness for the adulterous act yesterday? As long as you stay in the adulterous "marriage", you will be tempted again and again to commit adultery. In fact, you are living in adultery and cannot inherit the kingdom of God (Yahuah). God (Yahuah) has to pull you out of that sinful life in order to bring you into the kingdom.

To obey this commandment of God to not commit adultery you must avoid anything which causes the lust of the eyes as well. Adultery begins with a desire which is nurtured until it manifests into action. Therefore nurture faithfulness for your spouse, daily. Say I love you to them and recognize each day they are a blessing you received from God(Yahuah).

If you are divorced, do not remarry or engage in sexual relations with another but rather dedicate the remainder of your life to the service of God(Yahuah) and the raising of your children. This might seem a bit difficult for a single divorced mother of three children but it is a way that God(Yahuah) will be able to bless you. You won't be alone if you make God (Yahuah) your refuge.

If you are in a "marriage" after a "divorce", then you have to end this extra "marriage." This is not easy but you must choose this day, life or death, heaven or hell and destruction. The choice is set before you. True repentance for this is necessary in the heart of the believer. The Poverty CURSE is always a threat to persons in this adulterous relationship and only the mercy of God(Yahuah) keeps it from its full fruition.

Why all the fuss about adultery?

Because in the scripture God (Yahuah) compares his relationship to his people, his congregation, as a marriage.

When the people left him to worship other gods, it was compared to the act of committing adultery against their husband, Yahuah. This is the spiritual aspect. And so in our human life, adultery is also a serious matter. It serves as a warning to men and woman against treating their partners as objects to be used and discarded when no longer desirable. Marriage is sacred and the relationship is life-long "till death do us part." No adulterers (spiritual or earthly) will inherit the kingdom of heaven.

In Revelation 2:22 we see it is written, "Behold, I will cast her into a bed, and them that commit adultery with her into great tribulation, except they repent of their deeds." This is speaking of religious adultery. But if one can repent of this adultery in order to avoid tribulation, then one MUST repent of fleshly adultery against one's spouse in order to avoid the wages of sin.

What if a couple divorces then a month later the ex-husband dies, can the woman remarry? Yes. In the eyes of heaven she is a widow not a divorcee. A widow or widower is free to remarry.

Suppose there are two couples(A & B) who divorce and a month later the ex-husband in couple A dies. Can the ex-husband of couple B marry the widow A? No. That would be adultery because couple B are not divorced in accordance with heaven's rules.

8. Thou shalt not steal *(Exodus 20:15)*

Do not take anything which is not yours. Sometimes organizations charge people for items that are essentially worthless. This is stealing from people.

Churches with ministers who tell their poor and needy congregation to give and give so that God (Yahuah) can bless them, while the minister lives in a million dollar home is stealing from the poor. Credit card interest, national debt interest of countries, and inflation are all other forms of theft from the people.

On a personal level, if you take a paper clip from the workplace that is not yours, you are stealing from your employer. If you did that in the past unknowingly, then all you can do now is seek forgiveness and move forward in honesty and truth. When a person does work for you and you refuse to pay them the price you agreed upon, that is stealing too. These bring the CURSE of poverty upon the land.

Here is another form of stealing. Let's say your employer is paying you $20 per hour to do a job. One of your assigned tasks should take you no more than 1 hour to do but you stretch the job out to take 3 hours so that you can be paid $60. That is stealing your employer's money.

I know one gentleman who told me he does this sort of thing. I was completely disgusted by this and told him it's not right. I once had a contractor working on a job for me at a predefined rate. I caught her surfing the internet, playing on facebook, and checking out her linked-in profile instead of doing the job I was paying her for. When I told her about it, she made excuses.

Since I had already paid her for the period, I suggested that she make up the extra time to me. Later on she quit the project. Years later, she approached me again to work for me. I told her she was dishonest, untrustworthy, and ungrateful because she stole my money and did not fulfil her obligation. I told her I would consider hiring her again if she met certain conditions I had to prove her trustworthiness. She never replied to me. She was still a dishonest person.

The housing implosion was due to the sale of worthless Mortgage Backed Securities (MBS). The people selling them to the public were making tons of money on commissions while knowingly selling worthless items. It was theft of people's money but it was legal. Morally and in the kingdom of heaven, it is totally unacceptable and God (Yahuah) sees it for the theft that it is.

The government should have done right by those honest people who lost their money and had those criminally greedy traders put in jail. Yet, no arrests were made in America save 1 person. And the American people got no bailout money. Thus, no justice was administered in the earthly realm. However, if any of those children of God (Yahuah) wronged by the theft petition the kingdom of heaven for justice in the matter, it can open up an abundance of CURSES upon those responsible for the fraud and theft of the money.

Where humans fail in justice, heaven will not fail.
In order to keep this command, it is very important to be conscious of your dealings with others. Since theft involves another person, you have to be honest in your actions, words, and deeds. If you do slip up and steal from someone then go to them and make amends. Repay the money that was taken from them or provide the service you promised to do and add extra at no cost. Then you can take a step to avoid the Poverty CURSE.

9. Thou shalt not bear false witness against thy neighbour. (Exodus 20:16)

If you write or speak anything about your neighbour which is not true, you are opening the door for the CURSE unto yourself. Even repeating the truth about someone in order to defame his or her character, is breaking this command. Jesus(Yahusha) did not openly accuse Judas of theft or betrayal, even at the moment when Jesus(Yahusha) was arrested, but yet called Judas friend, until the end. The Bible also says that Michael the archangel when battling for the body of Moses did not bring a railing accusation against Satan but said, the Lord (Yahuah) rebuke you.

Bearing false witness can also be things like bringing false accusations against a person in order to derail their good name when you know it is not true.

Bearing false witness can also be bringing up a wrong done to you 20, 30, or 40 years ago against a person in order to destroy their character or to gain some secret monetary compensation.

Suppose a person (A) did a wrong act 20 years ago but they are now living a godly life, keeping the commandments, and showing mercy and love to others. Suddenly the wronged person (B) brings a scathing complaint against the person (A). Can this be wrong? Yes.

If the person (A) has been living a godly life, then they are not the same person who committed the wrongful act 20 years ago. They have changed. It is wicked to attempt to extract justice from person (A). However, person (A) should do something to help person (B) overcome their hurt and seek reconciliation in truth, mercy, and love.

One example is the apostle Paul. Before he was Paul, he was Saul the persecutor of the followers of Jesus (Yahusha). He was even given authority to kill believers. Saul was feared and hated. He was responsible for the death of good people. Yet, once he had a conversion of heart through his relationship with Jesus (Yahusha), he was no longer the same character of Saul.

He was now the character, Paul. His gospel ministry spread the good news far and wide and even across time to our present day. Would it have been right for a person (B) to come to Paul five years into his ministry and accuse him of killing their uncle and demanding justice? No.

Paul was no longer Saul though the DNA was the same, the heart, mind, and soul was transformed and made new. So to accuse Paul is to bear false witness against the new creature God(Yahuah) had created.

Here's another example. Jezebel was the queen and wife of king Ahab. She was a wicked queen but she was loyal to her weak husband, Ahab. Ahab wanted (coveted) a piece of land owned by an honest gentleman. The honest man refused to sell the land to the king. The queen saw Ahab sad and asked him what's the matter.

When she heard it, she told Ahab don't worry, he will have it. She had her people bear false witness (lie) against the honest man accusing him of blasphemy (heresy). The honest man was then taken and stoned to death. Then the queen went to the family and bought to land for Ahab. This is wicked.

Today, the corporate controlled media is used to bear false witness against people who are innocent. Sometimes even reporting an "alleged" crime is just as bad as bearing false witness because the character of the person is damaged even after they were found to be innocent of the alleged wrongdoing.

The corporate media as well as social media are two large sources of risk of bearing false witness. This opens the possibility of the Poverty CURSE impacting millions who repeat a falsehood by talking or by clicking and sharing or forwarding it.

To keep this commandment, only live in compassionate truth.

10. Thou shalt not covet thy neighbour's house, thou shalt not covet thy neighbour's wife, nor his manservant, nor his maidservant, nor his ox, nor

his ass, nor any thing that is thy neighbour's. (Exodus 20:17)

To obey this rule, you must not allow yourself to become jealous of anything that anyone has. Be contented with whatever you have. Catalogues, window shopping, advertising are all ways to remove your contentment and get you to covet.

A marketer's job is to create discontentment in you and create the illusion that what they are advertising will give you contentment. However they put it another way: they say they are solving your problems. Thus the marketing profession is about getting you to covet in one way or another.

How about whiter teeth? Marketing tells you that your smile must be white like the movie stars. You covet their big bright white smiles. And marketers have the solution for you with toothpaste X or cream Y. Never mind that in nature no person has bleached white teeth naturally in their mouth. Toilet paper is another created need for example. You can't imagine yourself without toilet paper, correct? But in some South Asia countries, they use soap and water to clean after using the toilet which is actually more hygienic than toilet paper. It also saves trees. Marketing has turned toilet paper into a solution to a manufactured problem. But what was the original problem it was trying to solve? I'll leave that for you to ponder.

I'm publisher of a magazine in Toronto so I know how ads work. Ads play on your emotions and rarely speak to your rational mind. Thus you must develop mastery over your emotions so that your emotions are not exploited to get you to covet things you really do not need. There is so much information I can share about this which you need to know. My online course has access to more information that will help. You'll learn more about it at the back of the book.

To keep this rule, be thankful daily for what you do have. Train your mind so that no external advertising force will be able to remove your contentment. Prayer and lots of mindful meditation may be required.

Jesus (Yahusha) also gave two great commands.

1.Love the Lord your God (Yahuah) with all your heart.

This rule is so simple that a child can easily understand it. Perhaps that is why adults tend to stumble with this rule. What does it mean to love with all your heart? Ask any mother who is willing to sacrifice for her child and you will know what it means to love with all your heart. Loving God (Yahuah) with all you heart is being willing to sacrifice if needed. However, Jesus (Yahusha) says, come to me… my burden is light.

When you sacrifice for the God of all creation, it may seem like you lost a lot but you actually receive more than you gave up because he knows your sacrifice out of your poverty while he gives out of his abundance. If you gave the Queen your best gift, it could never be rich enough but if the queen gave you one of her lesser gifts, it would still be highly valued. It's like that with the kingdom of heaven but on a much grander scale.

2.Love your neighbour as yourself.

Most people know how to love themselves. It is only in rare instances where people have grown up in the most terrible environment that they don't know how to love themselves. What does loving yourself mean? Is it chasing pleasure? Is it avoiding pain? Is it about getting the best for you no matter who you have to step on?

Heaven forbid. Loving yourself is about having a knowledge of your own worth AND understanding of the purpose and meaning you bring to the lives of those around you. It is knowing why you exist and living in that truth. When you understand that and you recognize that others are just as worthy as you are of love, compassion, and a helping hand, then you will be following the rule of loving your neighbour as you love yourself.

Obey ALL the commands and take another step toward Freedom from the CURSE.

* * *

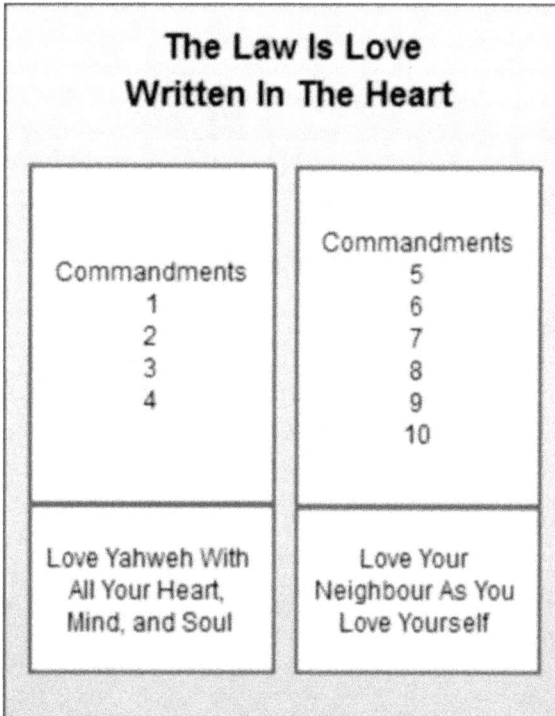

The Law Is Love
Written In The Heart

Commandments 1 2 3 4	Commandments 5 6 7 8 9 10
Love Yahweh With All Your Heart, Mind, and Soul	Love Your Neighbour As You Love Yourself

Course Note: The law of God (Yahuah) is about love. The ten commandments written by his finger into stone speak to how to love him, and how to love our fellow humans. In the course, we mention how this love has played out in history and how it is playing out now in our modern time. We also speak to connection between the LAW and the CURSES. Write your notes from the course below.

_____

_____

_____

_____

_____

_____

_____

_____

It is interesting to note that these factors can affect anyone regardless of skin colour, race, ethnicity, or gender. Note the majority of the factors are man-influenced. This means that human beings also have the capacity to fix the poverty CURSE problem if their hearts, minds, and spirits were in the right place. Where you do you see yourself on this spectrum?

* * *

Stop And Think

Don't just rush into the next chapter. Explore how reading this chapter has made you feel.

Realization: Now I understand these 10 universal laws and their relation to the CURSE, I see how I've been in violation. I now know that the Creator of the universe is on my side and His rules are not difficult to follow. In obedience there is power to shield me from the CURSE.

Prayer: Glorious Father, I now see that I've been violating your laws and opening the doorway to the CURSE. Please forgive me for my trespasses and disobedience of your laws. Grant me your Spirit of Truth to know to do right and the courage to do it. Break this generational CURSE for your name sake. I give you praise, honour and glory for your loving intervention in our lives, by giving us these divine laws. Please fill my life with your love and help me share all you teach me with others around me. Blessed be Yahuah, God Almighty. Amen.

Affirmation: Today I pledge to keep the Ten Commandments plus two.

* * *

Go to checkpoint #7:
www.breakthepovertycurse.com

Write Your Personal Insights Here

_____

_____

_____

_____

_____

_____

_____

_____

_____

_____

* * * * *

In our course on Breaking the Poverty Curse at Berkeley
Academy, we tackle the topic in more details and give you
more fast start money ideas for your cash flow situation. You
are simply lacking in some core aspects of fast cash seeding
and reaping. Check out the course at
http://berkeley.academy/our-courses/

* * * * *

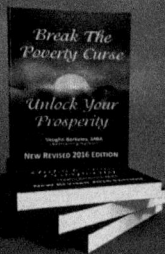

Righteous Dealings (Awakening)
Chapter 8

* * *

For I know the thoughts that I think toward you, saith the LORD, thoughts of peace, and not of evil, to give you an expected end. Then shall ye call upon me, and ye shall go and pray unto me, and I will hearken unto you. And ye shall seek me, and find me, when ye shall search for me with all your heart. - Jeremiah 29:11-13

A budget is telling your money where to go instead of wondering where it went. - John C. Maxwell

When you begin to open your eyes to money, it hurts at first, like coming out of a dark room into a bright room hurts your eyes, but when your perception adjusts you will be amazed at how different the world looks. ~ Vaughn Berkeley, MBA

* * *

The previous chapters dealt with many Spiritual elements of the CURSE of poverty. These are foundational concepts which must be understood if you seek true relief from the Poverty CURSE.

The following chapters will give you the basic financial tools and understanding you need, to climb out of the pit and from under the CURSE of poverty. It is not a get rich quick guide, so if you were looking for easy money, you are mistaken. Diligent work without the influence of the CURSE, will produce enduring prosperity which is what you ultimately desire.

Financial Knowledge You Need to Know

Income: In layman's terms, this is the flow of substance into your possession. That flow may be cash, gifts, donations and blessings from God (Yahuah).

Sources of Cash Income include:
o Salary from Employer
o Commissions
o Interest from savings
o Dividends from shares
o Self employed income (Sale of Services)
o Income from business activities (Sales)

Types of Income include:

Active Income
This is income based on the continuous exercise of your effort. No effort = No income.
Examples of this income include:
- Working for an employer.
- Begging / Pan handling for money.
- Any self employment activity that ceases to earn income when you are unable to work.

Passive Income
This is the income you earn from a one time investment in a project and it pays you afterwards with minimal work.
Examples of this income include:
- Creating/selling books, music, movies
- Vending machines
- Software programs
- Automated car washes

Residual Income
This is income that you earn on a repeated cycle. Your effort is exerted once in a big way to get the ball rolling, and then in smaller increments to keep the funds flowing.

Examples of this income include:
- Service Level Agreements (SLA)
- Insurance Commissions
- Educational Fund Commissions
- Subscriptions
- Rental Income
- Monthly memberships
- Usury (Condemned by God)

When you are just starting out, you must apply yourself to getting income from the active stream if you have no other avenue. However, you should never remain in that stream your entire life. You must find a way to move your income generating activity into the passive and residual streams, in order to prepare for yourself as you get older.

This enables the type of prosperity that God (Yahuah) wants for us all. When we plant a tree, we don't get one fruit only. We get many fruits with many more seeds. A one time investment of digging the soil and planting the seed and tending the seedling, leads to continuous payoff over the life of the tree. You need to find you own way to create residual income. The income potential is almost infinite.

Ponder this point: What if someone told you that you could make $50 every month and you didn't have to work for it? Would you take that? I would. If you didn't need to use any more of your time, your money, or your scarce resources and were able to make an extra $50 every month. Over the course of 50 years that is roughly $30,000. It not a huge amount of money for 50 years. The beauty of this is that it cost you no extra time or money to earn it. And what if the person told you that you could have 10 income generating things that each earn you a maximum of $50 per month for 50 years(600 months). Now the math looks better. It is: 10 items X $50 X 600 months. That's roughly $300,000 that did not require you to add more of your time, your resources, or your money to earn it. The KEY is not to focus on the $300,000 BIG PAY OFF. That's how wicked people entice others into get rich quick schemes. Instead focus on that $50 every month that flows like a little river.

I've created a series of ultra-short instant download reports called The Side Hustle Chronicles. They describe just one business idea and go into deeper instructions about that one single idea. That's all. You read the side hustle that interests you and you decide if you could make a go of it. Plus I have created some income reports that talk about this or that side hustle so you can read the actual income report and decide if it's right for you. Simple right? Yes. And it is my hope to create more of these as time progresses for the benefit of my people.

I've priced these very cheap. It's like you're basically buying me a Starbucks coffee in order to pick up some gems this way. I think that's reasonable considering the amount of time and energy I put into these for my tribe. Here are some quick links:

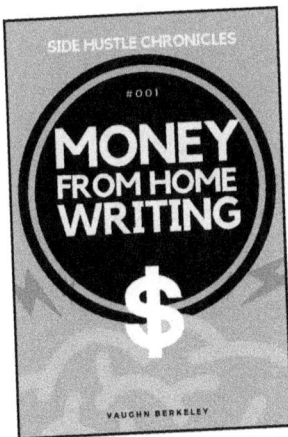

Customer/Buyer Testimonial

"I loved this report Vaughn. It was so detailed and in-depth. I was able to read and really follow along with this side hustle. Thanks for putting this together."

Available on
http://88deals4u.com

This book is available as a PDF and you can download and read it in an evening. Then you can decide if this option for writing from home will work from home. I would suggest you get this one if you have a passion for writing. If you don't like writing then don't even bother to get this side hustle. There are other types of side hustles and if you browse through it, you might find something that appeals to you.

Income Report
March 2017
Order your Copy at 88deals4u.com

Income Report
April 2017
Order your Copy at 88deals4u.com

Income Report
May 2017
Order your Copy at 88deals4u.com

These are a few income reports that are available for the Side Hustle Chronicle on making money writing from home.

These very inexpensive reports are great to give you sneak peak into whether this is right for you.

Available on
http://88deals4u.com

Expenses: In very simple and layman's terms is the flow of substance away from your possession.

Sources of Expenses include:
o Income Taxes
o Phone Bills

o Credit Card Debt (Expense)*
o Line of Credit Debt (Expense)*
o Travel expenses
o Rent
o Mortgage (Debt) expenses**
o Interest Charges on Loans**
o Tuition Fee expenses
o Textbook expenses
o Groceries expenses
o Television expenses
o Entertainment expenses
o Clothing expenses
o Retirement Savings Expense (RRSP in Canada)
o Disposable Asset Expenses***

The following is estimated based on the information that you have entered.

Province	Tax Bill	Tax Freedom Day	Days Worked For	
			The Government	Yourself
Newfoundland	$35,402	July 5	185	180
Prince Edward Island	$28,877	June 1	151	214
Nova Scotia	$30,406	June 9	159	206
New Brunswick	$28,862	June 1	151	214
Quebec	$32,861	June 22	172	193
Ontario	**$29,036**	**June 2**	**152**	**213**
Manitoba	$29,026	June 2	152	213
Saskatchewan	$31,387	June 14	164	201
Alberta	$26,504	May 20	139	226
British Columbia	$29,843	June 6	156	209

Recalculate   *(Ref: 2008 Calculation, in First Edition)*

Of the expenses listed above, there are good, neutral or bad ones. This is not a moral condemnation or approval of any item on the list.

Moreover, I must say, that I don't expect a servant of our wonderful Messiah (Yahusha), to be part-taking of the bad items. Good expenses are the ones that you expend today, which assist you in preparing for a better future.

217

Some of the good expenses would include tuition, retirement savings expense and the principle portion of a mortgage expense. Why would these be classified as good? When you pay tuition fees, it is in exchange for an education that will assist you in earning a better income later on in life. This is

(2016, 70K Salary, Married, 1 Child) Province	Tax Bill	Tax Freedom Day	Days Worked For	
			The Government	Yourself
Newfoundland	$31,716	June 15	167	199
P.E.I	$28,526	May 30	150	216
Nova Scotia	$29,416	June 3	155	211
New Brunswick	$30,563	June 9	161	205
Quebec	$30,546	June 9	161	205
Ontario	**$28,363**	**May 29**	**149**	**217**
Manitoba	$28,802	May 31	152	214
Saskatchewan	$27,023	May 22	142	224
Alberta	$24,328	May 8	128	238
British Columbia	$28,847	May 31	152	214

good because you have hope for a better future with it. Retirement saving expenses represent another good expense, because it is putting away money for your future, so that, once you are past your active earning age, you will be able to live off the savings.

The principal part of the mortgage expense is good, because it is tied directly to the value of your house. The interest component is a bad expense, because it is robbing you of your wealth. Its destructive force increases exponentially with time. I've discussed it in greater details in later pages of this book. Other expenses which take away your money for short term gratification or pleasures can be very bad.

Assets: These are accumulated, and usually hold good income generating capacity for you. Assets are enablers of your prosperity and wealth. Assets can be tangible such as your computer, car, furniture, etc. or intangibles like your educational skills and reputation and your relationship to God (Yahuah).

Liabilities: These are items which drain your prosperity away. They can be accomplices in keeping you under the CURSE of Poverty.

Usury/Debt: This is without a doubt the nuclear weapon of the CURSE of poverty. It is a weapon of mass destruction with a history of proven effectiveness over thousands of years. If you get mixed up in this, you'll find yourself under the CURSE no matter which side you are on. This device kills both the initiator and the target. If you are a lender, you may as well think of yourself as a spiritual suicide bomber. If you build your wealth on debt, you've built your house on sand.

Exodus 22:25	Leviticus 25:35-37
Deuteronomy 23:19	1 Kings 4:1, 7
Nehemiah 5:5-11	Psalms 15:1-5
Proverbs 28:8	Ezekiel 18:5-9
Matthew 18:32-35	

Note the key points of each verse below:

_____

_____

_____

_____

_____

_____

_____

_____

Taxation: This is an attempt to redistribute wealth from the middle class to the very poor and the wealthy. A progressive or graduated income tax is a plank of the communist manifesto. Its aim is to rob from the ignorant middle class and redistribute that wealth to the rich via their tax breaks, and distribute some crumbs to the poor, in an attempt to justify the system. Income taxation robs the working man of his hard earned wages, period.

Back in 2007/2008 while working on the original edition of this book, I was amazed by the Frazer Institute's tax freedom calculator. According to a personal tax freedom calculator on the Fraser Institute's website (http://www.fraserinstitute.org/tools/default.htm), a person making $70,000 a year in Ontario would work for the government for 152 days and only begin working for himself on June 2 of that year.

The image above is from the 2008 calculation I did. However, that tool was not on the Fraser Institute website when I looked when I started recreating this new edition of the book. However, God(Yahuah) was good and I found the tool again on its own domain. This is useful just to have an idea of how many days you work for the government before you actually begin to work for yourself. It's the length of days of your enslavement each year.

I ran the calculation again to see how the numbers looked in 2016. This time I ran the calculation for a married person making $70,000 per year with one child. On the new chart, you see that the days worked for the government is 149 days in Ontario in 2016.

With this knowledge and this tool, you can begin to speak to your accountant about possible tax advantages available to you in your current status in life. Perhaps there are a few items which you are not taking advantage of which you need to begin to do from this year.

The more you, as a believer, can get some of the allowed tax relief available, the easier it is for you to have more money to spend on helping the poor, or supporting a ministry or charity that does the work that is aligned with your heart.

Tax Freedom Tool Link: http://www.taxfreedomday.ca/

Remember, taxation is a form of economic oppression on the middle class, in an attempt to place persons there, under the CURSE of Poverty. God will repay this act Himself. Honest work by a person entitles that person to the full reward of their labours.

Malachi 3:5	Luke 10:6-7
1 Timothy 5:18	2 Kings 23:33-37
Daniel 11:20	Luke 18:10-14
Luke 19:2-8	Matthew 17:24-27

Note the key points of each verse below:

_____

_____

_____

_____

_____

_____

_____

Jesus(Yahusha), our wonderful redeemer, told the parable about the pastor and the tax collector. The parable reflects that both were praying in the temple. The pastor was praising himself in his prayer to God (Yahuah) and listing all his good qualities. Don't we know a few folks like that?

The pastor then observes the tax collector, and intones that he's not like that sinner. The tax collector on the other hand was praying sincerely, and with all his heart asking for God's (Yahuah) forgiveness and help.
Jesus(Yahusha) then said that the tax collector's prayer was honoured by God(Yahuah) and the pastor's was not.

I believe there are sincere and good people working for the tax collection agencies. Unfortunately, many of them neither know nor understand, the way the Poverty CURSE is linked to this profession. Thus, they are unintentionally opening the doorway for spiritual CURSES to come upon them in this profession.

As a believer in our God(Yahuah) we should not join this profession as a career even if the job is a good paying and stable job. It is not a job appropriate for the one in whom the Spirit of God(Yahuah) is working to create his image.

Zacchaeus was a chief tax collector, who had a personal experience with Jesus. Jesus(Yahusha) actually went to his house and visited. Zacchaeus told Jesus that he gives half his possession to the poor, and if he took anything by false dealing from anyone, he repays four times the value. Jesus(Yahusha) assurance to him that he was in good standing with God(Yahuah), speaks to all tax collectors today who hear His voice. I know that God(Yahuah) is speaking to them via this book, calling those who would have everlasting life.

Inflation: This is a hidden tax on everyone whether rich or poor, via the debasement of the national currency. The purchasing power of your money gets eroded over time, as a result of deliberate acts, on the part of those entities who control the debt-based monetary system of a country. It is a direct result of engaging in a debt-based economy and fractional banking.

According to the calcxml website, if you bought a basket of goods for $100 in 1950, that same basket of goods in 2014 would cost you just over $980. We're not talking caviar here. We're talking about an ordinary basket of goods that ordinary people would eat in 1950. Fruits, veggies, bread, canned foods might be examples of those things in that basket.

This inflation in the cost of these basic goods is a major reason why young people cannot get ahead in our society today. Ordinary things are costing them so much more money than their parents and grandparents and these young people are not the cause of the inflation. They are bearing the burden of their parents and grandparents.

Is it possible to beat inflation so that you are coming out ahead of the system rigged to cause you to fail?

Well, if we think of it this way, we might find a clue to that answer. Suppose you had a wooden bucket. A very strong neighbour came to you and drilled a hole mid way up your bucket and told you if you plugged the hole, you'd get a severe beating. Now every time you fill your bucket with water from the well, the top half leaks out through the hole and you are left with the bottom half for yourself. What can you do in that scenario?

You could go to the well and fill your belly with water then fill your bucket with water and run home as fast as you can with a belly full of water and a leaky bucket. I think you would agree that is an exercise in frustration. Sadly, most people live their lives just like that year after year.

Your other option is to arm yourself with knowledge of how to obtain a new bucket or even to flow water from the well to your house and eliminate the bucket completely. This is the way most people do not choose. Thus most people are living lives with a leaky bucket.

Is there a way to beat inflation? You cannot stop the system but you can use wisdom to minimize the impact to you and your family. My book on the food supply and our total reliance on it is a great starting point for you. The book is called Fresh Food4Life: The Case for Taking Back Control of Your Food and Empowering Your Family and Community.

Use the calculator to check out for yourself what $100 would have been worth in the 1970s, 80s, or 90s.

Source:
https://www.calcxml.com/calculators/bud12?skn=#results

Fractional Banking and Fiat Money: Fiat money is paper money not backed by anything. The only thing that gives it any value is the faith of the people that it is worth something. This faith is manufactured by the government endorsement of the currency which causes people who trust their government to trust the currency.

The central bank and her daughters, the public banks, employ fractional banking to create money out of nothing, but demand interest in the blood and sweat of the people.

Keynes (1919) explained that fiat money and inflation "gradually reduces the standard of living by secretly confiscating the income of the citizens and transferring it to the owners of the central bank that does the confiscating."

Thus, any country that uses this system is enabling the CURSE upon its citizens.

Josiah Charles Stamp, former director of the Bank of England once stated,

"The bankers own the earth. Take it away from them, but leave them the power to create money, and with the flick of the pen they will create enough deposits to buy it back again. However, take it away from them, and all the great fortunes like mine will disappear and they ought to disappear, for this would be a happier and better world to live in. But, if you wish to remain the slaves of bankers and pay the cost of your own slavery, let them continue to create money."

Exodus 19:5	Psalms 50:10-12
Amos 8:4-7	Leviticus 19:35-37
Proverbs 20:10, 23	Micah 6:9-15

Note the key points of each verse below:

_____

_____

_____

_____

_____

_____

_____

Fractional banking is the modern day equivalent of dishonest weights and measures. Understand this very important point. God(Yahuah) hates those who use dishonest weights and measures to rip off others.

In the quote I used earlier from Josiah Charles Stamp he claimed the banker will own the world. The bankers may be able to purchase property, but since the purchase is done through dishonest means, it invalidates the spiritual contract and initiates the CURSE. God (Yahuah) is the one who owns the whole earth, and allows kingdoms and people to dwell where He desires. When He says the meek will inherit the earth, He has power and authority to ensure it happens.

Loan Co-signer: A person who decides to become surety for another person. If the bank is unwilling to lend the original borrower without a co-signer, it's because they know that person cannot be trusted to repay. A co-signer then is the one the bank will go after. The Bible strictly forbids co-signing for anyone, and no Bible based believer should engage in co-signing for anyone. Never ask anyone to co-sign for you and never agree to co-sign for anyone. As a believer in the Kingdom of Heaven and a child of God(Yahuah), faithfully following his commands, statutes, and principles for wealth creation, you will have sufficient to rescue a family member in their moment of need.

Proverbs 6:1-2   Proverbs 11:15
Proverbs 17:18

Note the key points of each verse below:

_____

_____

_____

_____

_____

_____

_____

Budget: This is the tool that every man and woman should learn to master in their youth. Budgets are used by businesses to compare their financial performance to their plans.

For individuals, it is used to help us manage our inflows and outflows of our wealth. If you have never used a budget for your personal or business endeavours you are keeping yourself under the Poverty CURSE. It is a shame that schools do not teach this concept to children soon after children learn how to do their additions and subtractions.

It is possible that the educators themselves are ignorant of this principle for long term prosperity. You must learn how to effectively use a budget.

Luke 14:28-29

Tithes: This is an obligatory provision made to the priesthood of the increase from your fields. Every third year, this tithe was given to the poor, the needy, the widow, the fatherless, the stranger and the Levite. Some ministers remind church goers to bring in the tithe, but neglect to tell them that on the third year, their tithe should go toward those in need not to the church or pastors.

In our time, where most of us live and work in the city, your net income could be considered your increase, though some pastors would disagree. However, in my humble view, if you exchange your labour for money, then you really haven't made any increase assuming the exchange was fair.

If you own your business, the net income created after the expenses to produce that income would be your increase (profit).

On the point of giving to the poor, my grandmother used to prepare meals for the poor every couple of years to giveaway as a thanksgiving celebration and she was blessed for her entire life. She would invite community people to eat, and she had tons of food which was packaged and given to the poor. I don't even remember her working at a job a day in her life. Maggie, my grandmother, taught me this lesson from her living it in her life. I'm not sure if she fully understood the spiritual implications of her thanksgiving meal. She did it to bring blessings for herself and her children.

Deuteronomy 14:22-27 2 Chronicles 31:5-6
Deuteronomy 14:28-29 Deuteronomy 26:12-13

Note the key points of each verse below:

_____

_____

_____

_____

_____

_____

_____

If you obey this tithing principle, including the third year tithe for the poor, you will receive a guaranteed BLESSING of the work of your hands from heaven as the Bible declares.

Offerings: These are your free will gifts to the church for the furtherance of the gospel work. You give your offerings as you are able. They can be thanksgiving offerings, special occasion offerings, or offerings for specific church needs. Giving an offering helps deter the growth of greed or selfishness in your heart.

Acts 5:1-5

Year of Release: This biblical principle happens in the seventh year, when all debts are cancelled. The land was not harvested by the owner, but left for the poor and needy and animals to feast. This just and equitable redistribution of wealth based on God's plan was setup up so that God (Yahuah) provided for the owner for three years in the sixth year.

The owner would be blessed with sufficient for years six, seven and eight. Thus, the seventh year was truly a gift for the poor and needy who were not able to partake of the sixth year blessing. The release of the debtor was also a release from slavery. Debt is bondage.

A newly freed person could then turn to the fields to gain some increase to start a new life. This can be applied individually, by extending our charitable works in the year of release.

Deuteronomy 15:9   Leviticus 25:20-22
Leviticus 15:3-7

Note the key points of each verse below:

_____

_____

_____

_____

Jubilee Year: All debts are cancelled plus land sold would be transferred back to its original owner. This is a wonderful communal hedge against institutional greed and real estate exploitation.

People were not supposed to sell their inheritance land as it was a generational inheritance unless they came to such poverty that they had to sell. However in the 50th year, the land would be transferred back to them so their family inheritance would never be lost. The land had to be sold at a fair price to the original owner.

Christ(Yahusha) explained that there was even more, as he proclaimed in the temple, that the year included sight to the blind, the gospel taught to the poor, freedom to those in bondage and blessings without restraint.

Leviticus 25:8-19   Luke 4:18-21
Isaiah 61:1-6

Note the key points of each verse below:

_____

                                    .
_____

_____

_____

_____

_____

_____

To be in the presence of Messiah is to live in perpetual Jubilee. You need to read the gospels (Matthew, Mark, Luke and John) and understand the truths taught there to unlock your personal blessing and push back the CURSE. Seek the spiritual release offered immediately.

* * *

Course Note: In the course, we talk about using this grid and how it can be part of a system of awakening and motivation in your ongoing progress out of the POVERTY CURSE. Complete the grid according to the instructions given in the course.

Write your notes from the course below.

_____

_____

_____

_____

_____

_____

_____

_____

_____

_____

_____

* * *

Stop And Think

Once again we stop and consider all the knowledge gained in this chapter. Examine how reading this chapter has made you feel.

Realization: There are economic concepts that have been setup for my benefit, but there are also economic weapons designed to hurt me. Knowing the difference, and what the Bible teaches, can help me choose the good while avoiding the bad. I am thankful for the new knowledge, and the freedom from the CURSE it will usher in.

Prayer: Our Father in heaven, I am thankful for the financial and economic knowledge I've gained here. Please guide me into the wise use of these concepts to achieve spiritual, physical and financial freedom from the CURSE. I step forward in gratitude and faith this day. Blessed be Yahuah, God Almighty. Amen.

Affirmation: Today I will thoroughly understand these concepts and their application to me.

* * *

Go to checkpoint #8:
www.breakthepovertycurse.com

Write Your Personal Insights Here

_____

_____

_____

_____

_____

_____

_____

_____

_____

_____

_____

* * * * *

In our course on Breaking the Poverty Curse at Berkeley Academy, we tackle the topic in more details and give you more fast start money ideas for your cash flow situation. You are simply lacking in some core aspects of fast cash seeding and reaping. Check out the course at http://berkeley.academy/our-courses/

* * * * *

BERKELEY LIFE-BIZ PODCAST
With **VAUGHN BERKELEY** MBA, B.COMM

Featuring topics that help people live more productive lives, authors, entrepreneurs and more...

Listen on iTunes or on our website http://cmberkeleymediagroup.com

Season 1 is available free up on iTunes for you to listen. For details on new episodes, visit, cmberkeleymediagroup.com

Take Action

Chapter 9

* * *

The worst thing is to know what to do and not do it.

* * *

If you know the enemy and know yourself, your victory will not stand in doubt; if you know Heaven and know Earth, you may make your victory complete. - Sun Tzu

Like other gifts of God, the possession of wealth brings its increase of responsibility, and its peculiar temptations. How many who have in adversity remained true to God, have fallen under the glittering allurements of prosperity. With the possession of wealth, the ruling passion of a selfish nature is revealed. - E.G. White

If I can say that I have accomplished many things in life, it is because I have taken action, even when it seems like an impossibility. ~ Vaughn Berkeley, MBA

* * *

This chapter is entitled Take Action. It is not give action, or talk about action, or even look at action. It is about you, embracing action and taking it and making it part of your being.

You gain momentum. And I was inspired by no other creature than the humble and very active ant.

Why Study Ants

The wisest king on earth, under the inspiration of the Spirit of God, wrote in the book of Proverbs 6:6-8, "Go to the ant,thou sluggard; consider her ways, and be wise: which having no guide, overseer, or ruler, provideth her meat in the summer and gathereth her food in the harvest." King Solomon's kingdom was prosperous beyond any kingdom on earth. This wise king suggested we go to the ant to learn about industry. Even the Greek great thinkers like Plato, Plutarch, and Aristotle, praised the ant as a wise and clever creature. In this chapter, you'll get an orientation on ants and how they can help us break out of the POVERTY CURSE.

Story time: Many years ago my wife and I were driving down to Florida from Canada. It's about a 24-hour drive but we were stopping and sightseeing along the way so the trip took about four days. On the final day of the journey a funny thing happened with me and some ants. Just on the border of Florida, I needed to pee really bad. I was passing through a wooded area so I hopped out of the car and did the "I got to pee real bad" dance to a tree. I started to empty my bladder with great relief. Just as I was finished but before zipping up, I began to get bite after bite on my feet. I was wearing shorts and sandals and it seems I was on an ant hill. Now I began doing a "get off me dance" back to the car.

The bites from those ants stung. I always remember those tiny ants as my welcome to Florida with itchy/burning feet.

They were so tiny that I was not paying any attention to them as I was only thinking of my own need to empty my bladder. I was oblivious to their territory and their little community structure. Yet, they were well aware of my intrusion in their little part of the world.

It's funny now as I recall it but I had a great respect for their territory after the incident, I assure you.

The Social Structure of Ants

Ants have a social structure that is almost unique among living creatures. Only humans are similar to their structure.

Ants are an abundant life-form on the face of the earth. Scientists have discovered ants in most places on the earth. Ants are omnipresent on the earth. Scientists best estimate is that there are 10 million billion ants scattered across the surface of the earth. Their total body weight and mass represent 10% of all animal biomass on the planet. Their total weight is roughly the same as the entire human population. They are indeed plentiful and they prosper.

Ants have a highly developed social structure that allows them the benefits of freedom and cooperation, while maintaining a strict hierarchal structure. You have the queens, and the workers. The queen's sole function is to reproduce children for the colony. The workers, normally sterile females, are hardworking and caring for the colony. There are also males in the colony. The female workers, being sterile, would live life of eternal virginity; her only concern is for the care of her colony instead of the affections of a male.

Let's take a quick trip down the Bible to an incident with Martha and Mary when Jesus(Yahusha) had come over to visit. Jesus(Yahusha) was seated in the main room teaching everyone in the room about the mysteries of heaven. Mary sat close by Jesus(Yahusha) listening intently to every word from his lips. Finally, in her frustration, Martha, tells Jesus(Yahusha) that she has so much work to do in the kitchen and that Jesus should send Mary, her sister, over to help out with the chores. How did Jesus(Yahusha) respond? He told Martha that she was so worried and fretful about those things but Mary had chosen the better path and it would not be taken away from her. Read it in Luke 10:38-42. We will speak more on this as we work through this chapter.

Unity in Purpose

Ants don't have the burden of loneliness or depression. Life, for them, is about being part of the collective. A typical force may be 10,000 strong. Their collective strength allows them to lighten the burden of all while preparing the best possible odds of survival. It is impossible for you to learn from the ants if you are still stuck in childish selfishness. Selfishness is only about "me" or "#1". You won't be of benefit to a properly structured community if you don't embrace the unity of purpose for the greater good.

For the believer, this unity is created by a deeply held and treasured belief in the faith of God(Yahuah). Only when your heart is fully for God(Yahuah) and you are surrounded with others whose heart is fully for God(Yahuah) will you have the unity. This unity is in truth and the Holy Word of God.

Let's talk about those sisters Martha and Mary again. Martha and Mary did not seem to have unity of purpose in those moments leading up to Martha's complaint about being understaffed and overworked. But I ask you, which sister had the wrong purpose? Was it Martha who saw the group of people in her home and figured she needed to prepare a fresh cooked meal for about 15 people at least? Or was it Mary who ignored everyone's upcoming need to eat in favour of her purpose of just learning at the feet of the master? I want you to ponder this.

Rule #1: Build Together

Together, those wonderful ants build extraordinary habitats by working together. The little ants mound you see above the ground is only the tip of the iceberg, so to speak. Using their collective best interests, they work together to build an extensive underground network of chambers and passages. They maintain a constant connection with the community and allow for an optimal environment for peace, security, and for prosperity.

If you want to break the Poverty CURSE, you must be willing to build together with like minded ants like yourself. It means putting away the selfish "I" or "Me" mentality and trusting in the power of "We".

Here we are also taught about being in close proximity to each other when building your community.

Story time: Years ago, I happen to discover a small church group planted in a community they were trying to outreach to. Since I was curious about the church group and liked the idea of a small intimate setting rather than a big congregation, I attended regularly. The interesting thing about this group is that the only members from that community where the church was planted was me and my family. Everyone else who attended lived outside the region and basically came in for the weekend. Needless to say, it was a struggle for the group to fully integrate with the community where they were trying to win souls. The group failed one fundamental ant principle of building together and staying together. Being scattered in every direction made it almost impossible to be a member of that community. They wouldn't meet people while grocery shopping. They could not meet people while their children attended the school. Simple ordinary life activity opportunities were lost.

The lesson here is that if you want to work together as ants for the accomplishment of an objective of building together then make sure that you are living very close to your other ants members AND in the region where you desire to achieve your unified objective.

Rule #2: Sustain All, Protect All

Everyone has some kind of fantasy about this rule of ants. You see it frequently used in books and movies. Ever heard the saying, "All for one, and one for all"? That's from the Three Musketeers. How about the saying, "Ride or Die"? That's from the Fast and Furious movie franchise. These sayings speak to the concept that we are all working together toward the same goal.

Our efforts protect each other and our efforts sustain each other. In an era of individuality and selfishness, it is hard for people to understand this concept. They want people to be protecting and sustaining to them but are unwilling to reciprocate that with others.

It's like being in a relationship where one person decides they want to see other people but they want you to remain loyal to them. That's just pure selfishness and immaturity.

A sign of your maturity is when you are willing and able to keep the right attitude of being able to sustain all and protect all.

Shall we go back to our sisters, Martha and Mary for a moment? Okay. Did anything in their scenario give you an indication that they followed the pattern of sustaining all and protecting all? Actually, yes. When they opened their home for Jesus(Yahusha) and his disciples to stay and to be fed, they were living that principle. Remember Jesus(Yahusha) said in the scriptures that birds have nest, foxes have holes, but the son of man had nowhere. That was true. He was not a property owner. But with "ants" like Martha and Mary, he would always have a welcome place to rest when in their community.

Can this be applied to our modern day times? Yes. Suppose I was going to do a speaking gig or workshop in your city or any foreign city. I should be able to find a few believers there with the heart and means to allow me to stay by them for a week or even a month if I had a need. And there are people who accomplish this today. Some are not even religious and they exercise this principle. If more believers followed this principle, gospel workers would be able to move at liberty to where the gospel work was needed most. If you are suffering under the Poverty CURSE, then it could be a struggle for you to apply this.

Rule #3: Create New Members

The queen ant, is released from the burden of gathering food or building homes, or working because her task is to keep the numbers strong by breeding more workers. Jesus(Yahusha) said, "Go out into the world and make disciples." By telling you to make new members, Jesus was telling you to be like the queen ant. Create a new colony wherever you might find yourself. Even if you are not ready to disciple anyone, you can help someone already doing this function.

Are you able to create new members? How is your position in the Kingdom of Heaven? Have you studied to show yourself an approved labourer in the fields?

Many of us lack the tools to help others know of the love of God(Yahuah) and the Gospel ministry of Jesus(Yahusha). Thus, your option is to join with other "ants" who are working diligently for the kingdom.

Rule #4: Foster Vitality & Longevity

Insects have some of the shortest lifespans in nature. Their solitary nature expose them to dangers of starvation, the elements, predators, and failure to reproduce. It's a lot of hard work to survive in the world as an individual.

Ants tend to live longer because they have a division of duties that have allowed them to stack the odds in their favour.

To put that in a believer perspective, you cannot be a member of an "ant group" and you continue to poison your body with alcohol abuse or substance abuse. You can't consume the flesh of animals which leads to cancers, heart disease, and more. You have to treat your body as Holy and your vitality as critical to the success of your colony. Your lifespan is essential to the group/colony.

You've got to cut out smoking, drinking, drug use, sex addiction, or anything that diminishes your life force and vitality. You've got to switch over to a proper and well-planned vegan diet and lifestyle. You need to eat right, exercise, keep your mind active, and do these things because it is necessary for your health and the benefit of those of your colony who depend on you.

Let's talk about those sisters Martha and Mary again. Remember earlier I asked you to consider which sister had the wrong purpose. Was it Martha who saw the group of people in her home and figured she needed to prepare a fresh cooked meal for about 15 people at least? Or was it Mary who ignored everyone's upcoming need to eat in favour of her purpose of just learning at the feet of the master? It was Martha. Why? Because Martha was allowing the cares of this world to choke out her opportunity to learn from the Master, Yahusha(Jesus). If all Martha had was two flatbread and 1 portion of bean stew, Jesus(Yahusha) would have been able to perform a miracle to feed everyone with that portion. Thus Martha was fussing about something she really didn't need to because of her limitations of her faith. Mary on the other hand, had complete faith that when it was time to eat, there would be something.

Rule #5: Be Vigilant For Opportunities

Consider when one ant finds a source of food, she tells the others to come and get it for the colony. If you want to apply this principle, be on the lookout for deals and opportunities. When you find them, bring them to your "ant colony" to test it to see if it can benefit the colony. Everyone has the obligation to find good opportunities.

Maybe you have no means to be able to take advantage of a great real estate opportunity but a member of your group has the funds to purchase the property. Do you not tell them because you think they have enough money and you'll only get the crumbs? Heaven forbid. You bring the deal to them and ask them to give you a commission for finding you the deal.

If their heart is for the team, they will give you a commission and their increased resources will be of value to the entire colony.

Rule #6: Be Loyal To Your Colony

Ants live together as colonies. The members of the colonies are loyal to each other. They know that they are smaller and weaker than other creatures on the planet but they also know that there is strength in their unity. They are loyal to each other because their survival as a colony depends on it.

As a human, do you understand loyalty to your colony? Are you a member of a group that supports you like ants support each other? Do you have a family that is better than your own family?

The Christian has suffered persecution since the days of the Roman Emperors. Early Christians survived because they possessed the qualities of ants described above. They thrived because of the unity of the Spirit of God(Yahuah) working in them. Even during intense persecution, they were able to work together to keep the true word of God(Yahuah) moving forward throughout the ages.

Modern day secret societies and "brotherhoods" continue to thrive because they exploit this concept of secrecy and loyalty.

A true believer and follower of God(Yahuah) should NOT join any secret society. This is leaving yourself open to the POVERTY CURSE because your put your trust in them rather than in God(Yahuah).

The bible says you cannot serve two masters. You will love the one and hate the other. God(Yahuah) side does his works in the open not in secret.

Rule #7: Be Consistent

Ants have a consistency in their movement to a new area.
When they move to a new area and begin to colonize, you
will always see ants scouting around for food. They are
consistent in their mannerism.

Consistency is something that many people lack these days.
Unless you count being consistent in their inconsistency.
Many people will try one thing and realize that it does not
produce immediate results and so they drop it and move
onto the next thing.

In marketing terms, we say they have shiny object syndrome.
These types of people will try the latest money making idea
of this month. When they find out, it doesn't work as fast as
the gurus say, they lose interest in the following month.
Coincidentally, another marketer shows up with another
shiny object and they get seduced by that one. It seems like
what they really need and so they jump on that bandwagon.
It goes on and on like that producing no real results for
them.

The lesson for you is to be consistent in your effort over the
long haul. It took us four years to get the magazine,
EternityWatch, from 10,000 readers to over 120,000 readers
per quarter. But we have been doing the magazine for seven
years.

We might have been slower than other flashy magazines but
we were moving according to ants principles. Slow and
steady, and with a long term goal of continuity of the
message. We are in it for the long game.

How Can You Find Your Colony

It is very hard for some people to find a colony where they
can fit in and thrive. It must be based on a shared
fundamental belief system. For example, look at the vegan
movement in Toronto. It has grown and created widespread

influence because of the dedication of its members. Toronto Pig Save, an animal rights group, has operated under the ants principle though they are not a religious group. Their purpose is to expose the cruelty of the animal food industry by bearing witness to the transport trucks.

Anita, the leader (queen ant), is the one who is gentle and caring. Whenever you speak to her you feel an immediate connection to her. She's even been arrested for giving water to thirsty pigs on a transport truck on their way to slaughter. People can gravitate to her as a champion of animals.

There are many other volunteers who join their efforts to support the work of Toronto Pig Save by spreading the message on social media, selling stuff via the website, and getting sponsors for the various events and advertising activities.

I don't know how they afford food or pay rent because they seem to do activism full-time. It is only possible because of the ants principle. Someone else is creating the funds necessary to allow them the free time to do the activism work they do.

Thus, the ants principle, applied to any organization structure can create a significant and highly beneficial impact in the lives of all those connected to the organization where the principle is applied.

If you really want to begin to thrive, you need to become like the ant and seek a colony of ants where you belong and where you can fully thrive. Kind of like the people I keep around. I am always looking for good people with potential to do amazing things. I keep these people close to me.

This Is An Action Chapter

This is an action chapter so I guess I better give you some concrete action steps that you can apply to yourself.

First, memorize all the seven rules pertaining to ants. This is the very basic foundation but you must get it right before you can attain to higher levels of understanding.

Secondly, find yourself an "ant colony" where you belong. Today we use different words to describe them. We call them a tribe, a club, association, church group, committee, government office, activism group, or company. Don't look for a place that exactly matches where you are now. If you do that, you will stagnate and not grow as a person. You should find one that is where you want to be so that you can grow into the level you should be at. This is very important to remember.

Thirdly, if you want, you can apply to become part of my ants tribe. I am very selective of the people I allow into my tribe because the people you surround yourself with either bring out the best in you or they bring out the worst in you. I learned that the hard way by actually doing it.

I've been around people who were so negative and toxic that my joy and friendship was diminished around them. I've been around people who were like refreshing summer sunlight and gave me a boost just talking to them. I choose my ants tribe carefully because I choose to love those in my tribe. If you are interested, go to http://cmberkeleymediagroup.com/joinatribe to take the first step.

I've hardly mentioned the POVERTY CURSE in this chapter but it is so relevant to this chapter. The principles here are in place to help you learn how to operate under a new mindset. It is also for you to know how to build alliances to help you move forward.

* * *

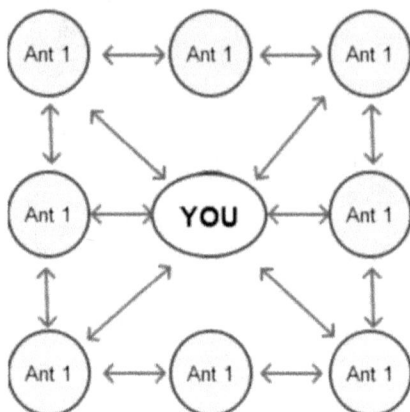

Course Note: In the course, we talk about the ant network as a support and survival mechanism. It is also useful to help lift all members out of the POVERTY CURSE. Complete the network according to the instructions given in the course. Write your notes from the course below.

_____

_____

_____

_____

_____

_____

_____

_____

* * *

Stop And Think

Don't just rush into the next chapter. Examine your emotions. Why do you feel this way? Can you really become free from the CURSE?

Realization: Now I understand truly how important it is to have a support group in place in my journey out of the CURSE. I have taken the steps in this chapter to move forward out of the curse.

Prayer: Almighty Yahuah, thank you for giving us the examples in nature to help us see principles we can use in our life. Teach me of you and your ways and the ants principles. Help me to follow you wholeheartedly. Renew my heart, my mind, my body and soul for you. Break this CURSE for your name sake. Thank you for loving me enough to intervene in my life at this present time. Please fill my life with your love and help me share all you teach me with others around me. Blessed be Yahuah, God Almighty. Amen.

Affirmation: Today I know the truth and I am finding my colony.

* * *

Go to checkpoint #9:
www.breakthepovertycurse.com

Write Your Personal Insights Here

_____

_____

_____

_____

_____

_____

_____

_____

_____

_____

* * * * *

In our course on Breaking the Poverty Curse at Berkeley Academy, we tackle the topic in more details and give you more fast start money ideas for your cash flow situation. You are simply lacking in some core aspects of fast cash seeding and reaping. Check out the course at http://berkeley.academy/our-courses/

* * * * *

The Money Dimension

IV

The Money Machine

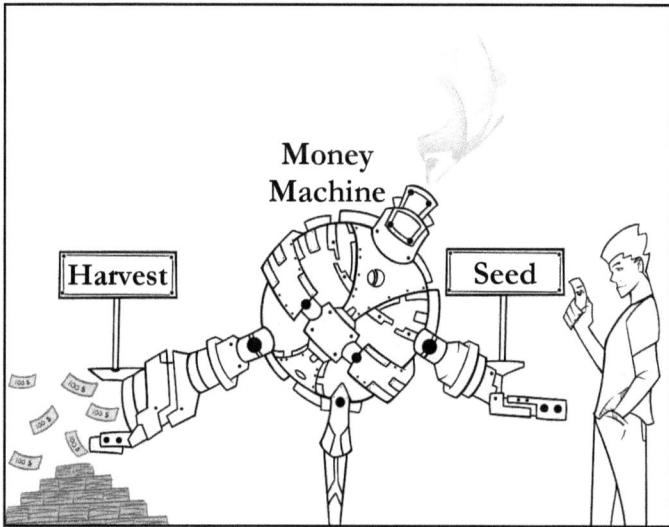

In this Money Dimension section of the book, we're going to become familiar with the practical aspects of earning to create prosperity while breaking the Poverty Curse.

Money Re-Education

Chapter 10

* * *

You've been misinformed your entire life.

* * *

Then said Jesus to those Jews which believed on him, If ye continue in my word, then are ye my disciples indeed; And ye shall know the truth, and the truth shall make you free. ~ John 8:31-32

There is no easy walk to freedom anywhere, and many of us will have to pass through the valley of the shadow of death again and again before we reach the mountaintop of our desires. ~ Nelson Mandela

The lies about money we believe are dangerous to our present life and future life. It is amazing to me that people don't question what they know to discover the truth. ~ Vaughn Berkeley, MBA

* * *

I want to open this chapter on a few of the thoughts that US President Lincoln expressed about money.

Abraham Lincoln's Monetary Policy, 1865 (Page 91 of Senate document 23.)

- **Money is the creature of law** and the creation of the original issue of money should be maintained as the exclusive monopoly of national Government.
- **Money possesses no value to the State** other than that given to it by circulation.

- Capital has its proper place and is entitled to every protection. **The wages of men should be recognised in the structure of and in the social order as more important than the wages of money.**
- **No duty is more imperative for the Government** than **the duty it owes the People to furnish them** with **a sound and uniform currency,** and of regulating the circulation of the medium of exchange **so that labour will be protected from a vicious currency,** and commerce will be facilitated by cheap and safe exchanges.

So what did you just read?

Money is only a creature of law. Money has no value to the Nation State. The wages of people must be recognized as more important than the wages of money (usury/interest).

Government has a fundamental duty to protect the labour and wages of men from a vicious or "criminal" currency. They understood the lowly position of money and the crooks who manipulate to cheat or steal from the honest labour of people.

Money Has Gone From Being A Worthless Phantom (Ghost) Into An Idol (Deity)

The Bible teaches the love of money is the root of all evil. Just think of this for a moment. Can you visualize your life without money? If you are like 99.9% of the population you probably cannot see your life without money. This is because such a life to you seems to be one of poverty and hardship or dare I say, HELL. Thus money has become a god that you must have in your life to save you from "hell". There are people who can visualize their life without Jesus(Yahusha) but they cannot see their life without money. Now that we have that mindset out in the open what are you going to do? Don't teach your children to idolize money. You must stop idolizing money.

Money is always around us and yet it has been kept a secret.
A secret hidden in plain sight. The 95% of the population
who remain poor never learn the secret. You can get a
glimpse into it by reading this book.

1.   Lie #1: Money for Hours Is A Fair Deal

Time is the most precious commodity we are given at birth
from our creator, God (Yahuah). Scripture teaches that we
are allotted 70 years as the average. This is equal to 613,200
hours. That's all. You cannot buy more time from God
(Yahweh). You cannot buy more time from others. You
cannot trade time. It is all you have so it is a scarce resource.
It should be immensely valuable to you.

Adam, the first man created by God (Yahweh) lived to be
over 900 years old. In Genesis 5:5 it states, "And all the days
that Adam lived were nine hundred and thirty years. And he
died." That's 8,146,800 hours! Got that? The first man had
930 years of life. That is a long time.

Today, all we have is a fraction of Adam's life span. Our 70
years on average up to a max of 120 if we are exceptional is
so small in the kingdom of God.

How can you or anyone think that wasting their life away for
minimum wage while not fulfilling the true purpose that
God (Yahuah) had planned for them is a fair deal? It is not a
fair deal at all. As long as you trade your extremely precious
time for money, you will be always undervaluing yourself.

God (Yahuah) asks that you voluntarily give him one day a
week of your time to have a relationship with you. That
works out to 87,360 hours. So technically, you only have
525,840 hours for yourself to do whatever you want. That's
even less and so very precious.

While doing the math I also realized that out of the 70 years
God (Yahweh) has given to humans, the total years He

offers for relationship with him is 10 years or 1 in 7. The same as the weekly cycle.

Will you keep wasting your precious time on social media? Will you keep wasting your precious time working at a dead-end job that will never allow you to achieve God(Yahuah) dreams for you? Will you keep wasting your precious time on self-pity, laziness, daydreaming, watching TV/Movies, or any activity that prevents you from actively moving toward the good life God (Yahuah) intended for you? Or how about exchanging your time for greed, a mental idol, if you're already wealthy?

Here's some truth for you: Trading your time for money, any inconsequential activity, or idol worshipping is not a good trade, EVER!

2. Lie #2: Using Credit Cards Are Smart

Most of the young people today don't remember a time before credit cards, but I do. I remember when you wanted something and couldn't afford it, you would put it on lay-away. Then you would pay monthly instalments until you paid it off then you could have the item from the store.

Sadly, with the onset of credit cards came the psychology of instant gratification along with deferred responsibility. Now people can pull out the credit card and buy what they want now, and don't stress out until the bill comes later. They are instantly gratified and they have deferred responsibility for the debt they incurred.

There was a science experiment done decades ago with children to test if they could delay instant gratification in order to get a better reward. A child was put in a room with a cookie. The child was told they could have the cookie now OR if they waited until the scientist returned in a while, they could have two cookies. Some children ate the cookie as soon as the scientist left. Other children distracted themselves by playing with some toy in the room, or other things to take their mind off the cookie. When the scientist returned, the child got two cookies. But the really interesting thing was that decades later, they found the children that had the ability to delay gratification were more successful in life while the ones who sought instant gratification were not as successful in life. Write this point down! The trait for success is taught from childhood. And it can be taught to adults as well.

Credit cards companies are causing people to seek instant gratification instead of waiting. The pattern of instant gratification, week after week, month after month, has a long term negative impact on the personal financial habits of the individual who is caught up in it. Do you know someone who carries a personal credit card balance every month? That person is being trained to practise financial failure and instant gratification.

Credit card companies are smart too. They charge the merchants a monthly "rental" fee for using the terminal machines plus a percentage of all sales they process. Then they charge customers high interest rates on purchases as well as annual fees for some cards. So basically the credit card company is making money off people at both ends of the transaction. It's like double dipping your chip in bowl of dip. Disgusting when you really think of it.

Sadly, most consumers use their credit cards to buy ordinary things that they could easily purchase with cash. Then they have to pay interest on credit card debt when had they been more careful, they could have avoided the charge completely.

Using a credit card to buy things you consume or use up is not a smart idea. Just pay for the item with cash. If you don't have cash to pay for it, save up for the item.

The Bible teaches that the borrower is servant to the lender. Put another way, you become a slave to the lender in order to do their bidding. Thus a believer should avoid the accumulation of debt.

3. Lie #3: When You Just Starting Buy A Fixer-Upper

Buying a fixer-upper property is the only way some people can break out of poverty and break into home ownership. Because new homes may be substantially more expensive than a poor person can afford, they are left with no other option but to buy a fixer-upper.

The problem with that is that the fixer-upper may require more money to fix it than the poor homeowner can afford. The amount of work required to repair the damage may be substantially more than the homeowner had anticipated.

Story time: A friend of a friend of mine was redoing his basement. He budgeted about $25,000 to do the renovations. As he was working with the contractor breaking down walls, tearing up the flooring to put down new flooring, guess what he discovered? He discovered layers of flooring from previous owners of the house. The house was very old so it was like a time capsule. Each layer represented when the previous owner just put down a new flooring on top of the old flooring.

There was sticky, gooey, stuff in the layers that this friend of a friend felt were a sure way to attract mice and roaches if not addressed. He instructed the contractor to rip up the old layers. This person wanted to do a good job because that is his nature. However, that added a few thousand more to the budget. It was more than he intended to spend.

That's the way it is with old homes that are breaking down. You may find years of half-done or poorly done patchwork which blows your budget sky high. You can save money by doing things yourself but you have to have the skills to make it happen.

For 9 out of 10 people, buying an old broken down, fixer-upper is a bad idea and a high risk option. If you read my book, Bringing your Heart Home, I talk about the housing deception that we are indoctrinated with from childhood.

I'm passionate about this topic and reading that book will definitely open your eyes. I also expose you to the real purpose of housing and how you should bring your heart home.

4. Lie #4: Entrepreneurship Is Hard

There are many people who tell you that entrepreneurship is difficult. One famous person, "Gary Vee" said he doesn't believe that everybody should be entrepreneurs. However, he made his multi-million dollars by being an entrepreneur. His thinking is that some people are just not cut out to be entrepreneurs and they actually will fail at it.

I agree that some people will fail at entrepreneurship but entrepreneurship is a skill to be mastered like welding or sewing or cooking. Everyone can learn it if they have a proper teacher or mentor to help them. Everyone can be an entrepreneur and I firmly believe that everyone should learn the skills to at least run a successful micro-business or side business or side hustle as young people call it.

The lie you've been led to believe that entrepreneurship is hard is because it is in the best interest of employers to have people who are satisfied with becoming worker bees or indentured servants. The person who is willing to stay in a job earning a survival wage for 20, 30, or 40 years, is the perfect kind of person employers seek.

For you, who are seeking a better position in life and seeking to break the POVERTY CURSE, it is important that you don't believe the lie no matter how many people echo it to you. Even if your mom and dad, tell you.

Entrepreneurship is a skill which can be learned and mastered by anyone, even a 10 year old kid.

5. Lie #5: Only Lucky People Make Money

This is one lie that some people believe in because of their own bad experiences with money.

Story time: A long time ago, I heard of a guy discussing money with another colleague. The guy said he had lost money before dabbling in investing and he seemed to be unlucky with money while his colleague seemed to have money falling on them from the sky. This made the person a bit sad and discouraged.

Others will tell you that the lucky people are the ones who have lots of money to begin with because they can find the good deals which other people without money cannot find. Some people might tell you that you need to forget about God (Yahuah) because God does not deal with money and so praying or believing in him for money is just a waste of time. The logic of that argument is that if the bible says the love of money is the root of all evil, then God(Yahuah) won't have anything to do with money.

The Bible tells us that God(Yahuah) has said all the earth is his property. He placed humans on here as stewards of his property. He gives wealth and the power to get wealth to those whom he desires in order to achieve his purpose.

Luck is a vapour that people are trying to make real. The reality is that by using the divine principles God (Yahweh) setup for the creation of long-term prosperity, you can reap the benefits. There is no such thing as luck. The "lucky people" who make money were simply applying a heavenly principle that they won't share with you. Like gravity, the rule will work the same for everyone.

6. Lie #6: You Need Money To Make Money

This is another lie that people are told by society. It is most often repeated by people without the skill, knowledge, or ability to make money. They are unable to make money so they make the next best thing in their mind: Excuses!

The skilful person in the art of the deal is able to make money without using a penny of their own money. They are able to find investors, find the deals, and create a win-win match. And they make money off the deal.

Stop believing in the lie that is fed to ordinary people all over the world. It does not take money to make money. It takes WISDOM to make money.

The Bible teaches that money is a defence and wisdom is a defence; but the beauty of wisdom is that it will preserve you where money cannot. There is a process to acquire wisdom and that is what you need to learn.

7. Lie #7: There Is No Way To Get Anything Without Money

This is a lie that is firmly rooted in most people. It is incomprehensible that a person can get something without money. Yet, as children, everything they have bestowed on them is a gift to them given from love. Most children do not have to go out and earn money in order to buy what they need.

If some children are learning to make money it is a hobby or side-hustle. Their parents are teaching them the value of entrepreneurship early on.

But you don't need to think that you cannot get anything done without money.

Ever hear of something called BARTERING?

This is where you trade someone something you have in exchange for something they have that you need. It's a pretty simple concept. And it has been tested in Canada with a very famous outcome.

A Canadian man started with a paper clip and he traded up each time until he ended up with a house. You can search online to find the story of how a paper clip became a house.

Now this is an extraordinary example of bartering at its best. And most people won't be able to achieve that. But what about being able to achieve part-time help for your micro-business? Or what about bartering some design services in exchange for your product? There's ways to make it work in the micro-economy.

The lie that you can't get anything without money is perpetuated because it is beneficial to all the people who make money off of people due to their own greed. I have even been known to barter with someone from time to time because it is sometimes a fun thing. You should not believe the lie but know the truth for yourself and learn the technique for bartering successfully.

There are three more points that you need to be re-educated on. But I'm making these points available via the 30-Day Email Coaching. If you're on the list you will get them when you get the lessons on Money Strategies. The email list for the 30-day email coaching will help you create some small wins. I really want people to internalize the lessons here.

If you didn't sign up for it yet for whatever reason, you should go to the web page listed in the back to find up how you can still get on the challenge.

* * *

L _____

I _____

E _____

S _____

Course Note: In the course, we talk about the acronym LIES and the significant it plays in your breaking free from the POVERTY CURSE. Complete the words according to the instructions given in the course.

Write your notes from the course below.

_____

_____

_____

_____

_____

_____

_____

_____

* * *

Stop And Think

Don't just rush into the next chapter. Examine yourself now. How does knowing the seven lies above make you feel? Why do you feel this way? Can you really become free from the CURSE?

Realization: Now I understand truly how important it is to not just believe the lies that have been taught to those before me. I must discover for myself where the truth is and how to use it in my life.

Prayer: Almighty Yahuah, thank you for giving me these seven principles of truth with regards to money. Help me to follow you wholeheartedly. Renew my heart, my mind, my body and soul for you. Break this CURSE for your name sake. Thank you for loving me enough to intervene in my life at this present time. Please fill my life with your love and help me share all you teach me with others around me. Blessed be the Yahuah, God Almighty. Amen.

Affirmation: Today I know the truth and I am restructuring my thoughts and actions based on the new truths.

* * *

Write Your Personal Insights Here

_____

_____

_____

_____

_____

_____

_____

_____

_____

_____

_____

* * * * *

In our course on Breaking the Poverty Curse at Berkeley Academy, we tackle the topic in more details and give you more fast start money ideas for your cash flow situation. You are simply lacking in some core aspects of fast cash seeding and reaping. Check out the course at http://berkeley.academy/our-courses/

* * * * *

Fast Start Money Ideas

Chapter 11

* * *

Some quick ways to get some quick cash.

* * *

None but those trained from youth to such an ordeal [the pressures and duties of royalty] can sustain it with amiability and composure. ~ Princess Alice, Countess of Athlon

The people curse him who withholds grain, but blessing is on the head of him who sells it. ~ Proverbs 11:26

Money loves speed and when you are starting out, you better learn how to hustle. Youth and vitality gives you an edge when you hustle. ~ Vaughn Berkeley, MBA

* * *

This is where the rubber meets the road. In my teenage years, I was a moneylender, and know how easy it was to make money from that system. I've also made money as an employee, an entrepreneur, and a consultant. I've also gained an understanding of micro-finance concepts in my later years. I'll share with you some simple strategies and other ideas that can start you on the path to producing income.

This chapter is for the person who is cash poor and wants to earn some money. Notice I didn't say make money but earn money. The only people who make money work in the mint. Be sure that some effort on your part is required. In attaining wealth, the flaws in your character will show, so take time to perfect your character as you go on this journey.

Buy Low, Sell High

Everyone has probably heard this concept some time in their lifetime. When you're in the CURSE of Poverty, your business must be able to run on a shoestring budget. Your expenditures must be kept low, while you attempt to earn more income. With the 2008 economic crash of the US and the world, it is became even more important to look for the cheapest ways to run your entrepreneurial enterprise. Back in 2008 in completing the first edition of this book, 18 banks had closed in the US and there were more. Thus you need to be prepared for tough times. Even if things seem better now in 2016, having a prudent fiscal strategy is always to your advantage.

Here are a few "Thou Shalt Not's" to cut expenditures:
1. Thou shalt not begin your business venture without seeking wisdom from God(Yahuah).
2. Thou shalt not jump into any MLM schemes without investigating the ones running it.
3. Thou shalt not arrange any long term leases for expensive locations or business equipment.
4. Thou shalt not invest thousands of dollars up front on any business venture no matter how sweet it sounds.
5. Thou shalt not hire employees or contractors until you can afford their salary for six to nine months or the duration of their assigned functions.
6. Thou shalt not throw money away on "scatter gun" advertising that generally doesn't generate leads which you can convert to a sale.
7. Thou shalt not take on huge debt to start your business. Your debt must be small and you should be able to pay it off if demanded of you.
8. Thou shalt assemble a good management team including the moneyman, the marketer, the lawyer, and the ideas guy. You should be one of the four but not all four. You only pay to use their services when you need it.
9. Thou shalt prepare a simple written business plan before you dive into your venture.
10. Thou shalt prepare a budget and use it.

When Warren Buffet, the great investor, looks at a company, he considers the integrity of the management team, the company cash flow, and the true value of the company.

Story time: I knew of a fellow who wanted to create his business. Let's call him, Jim. Jim told me when he first started, he opted a buy a truck from another fellow. The fellow was a trucker who had a few trucks so he was willing to sell one of his older trucks to Jim. Jim was fresh off the boat getting into this business and so he paid the fellow cash for the truck trusting that the fellow would transfer ownership of the truck over to Jim and use the money to bring the truck payments up to date which had fallen behind. Well, after a month, Jim gets a call from the finance company asking him about when the money was coming in to bring the truck up to date. Jim was shocked. He said he gave the fellow the money a month ago. Seems that nothing was paid on Jim's truck. Worst still, the truck was still owned by the fellow not by Jim. Jim called the fellow about it and he told Jim not to worry he was looking after it. Soon another call came to Jim. They were going to have to repossess the truck because of non payment. Jim was in a jam. As Jim was in the middle of a job, they allowed Jim to finish off his contract and then took the truck. Jim lost some money on that deal but thankfully he had made some money working the truck so it was not too bad. Jim should have had a few extra people on his team like the lawyer, the accountant, during this episode.

Even though your business is a small business, you must think of yourself as Buffet worthy in the future.

1. Ensure your management team is sound and righteous.
2. Keep your outflows of cash as low as possible while increasing your inflows.
3. Continuously build value for your business as each day, month and year passes.

Here are some examples and ideas:

Example 1: Street Selling Downtown

I have seen it applied in downtown Toronto. Some men in suits would stand out at the beginning of the each month with a black history month booklet they gave away in exchange for a donation. The booklet was roughly 10 sheets of paper stapled together. Let's see if this could be profitable:
Costs: $0.50 per booklet (5 cents x 10 sheets)
Average donation: $2.00 - $5.00
Profit per booklet: $1.50 - $4.50
They were in the centre of downtown Toronto in a high traffic area so the volume of sales was probably good. Therefore this business can be very profitable.

Example 2: Selling trinkets on eBay

I knew of a co-worker of mine who sold trinkets on eBay on the side. She created these pieces of art and sold them to make an extra income. Her costs were low and she was able to make a profit. A friend of mine, Jim, who also wrote for us in the magazine on wealth spoke about his teenage daughter making a great income on eBay. Way back in 2001/2002, I knew of a lady who sold stuff on ebay for someone. It was old war medals that the person bought and asked this lady to work as their administrative assistant listing the items on ebay. It was making money for the person who hired this lady to do the admin work.

Tutoring/Coaching

If you have knowledge or skills you want to share with others, then advertise your service. During my undergrad period of university, I made extra money tutoring foreign students in English, MS software tutoring and any other knowledge that someone was willing to pay me to learn. Can you use computer software well? Can you play a musical instrument? Do you have knowledge about building ant farms? I suggest you learn about yourself and your inner strengths, then see who is willing to pay you to learn it. Set a price that will cover your costs and give you a profit for your efforts. In our online course, we go into some modern day ways you can earn cash tutoring.

Find an Employer

Working for an employer may not be what you want to hear, but in the short term, you are exchanging your labour for some much needed start-up capital. If all else is difficult then this is by necessity your option. If you haven't used a resume then seek help in crafting a resume that presents your strongest attributes. Keep it updated quarterly going forward. The job is short-term so work hard at it with your ultimate goal in mind. Eliminate all non essential spending, so that your seed money can grow faster. Work at your best, knowing that God (Yahuah) is pleased.

2 Thessalonians 3:10-13
Ecclesiastes 11:6

Note the key points of each verse below:

_____

_____

_____

_____

Write a Book

Everyone has at least one good book inside of himself or herself. It may be a children's story or a poetry book or even a self help manual. Your life story may be even a point of inspiration for someone but you've got to tell it. There are people making rent money by writing books. Modern technology means low barrier to entry and big opportunity for authors.

Tips to get you started
1. Get a journal. Write daily for your book project.
2. Write at least an hour or more each day on your book..

3. Don't over analyze your book. You're not writing the encyclopaedia Britannica.
4. Keep at it until you're done.
5. Pray for the right words.

Upon completing your book, use the internet to find publishers or literary agents willing to work with you or alternately self-publish your book. If you plan to self publish, remember the up-front costs to you and ensure you have the cash to cover those expenses. They can be very hefty so have enough cash on hand for your upfront investment.

Do you think this is difficult? Well, I've been the personal writing coach to Jenny Berkeley, RN, CHN. She's published her first book in 2012 and by 2016, she has 5 published books and 1 in the pipeline due out in 2017. She's a bestselling author. She's met with a Prime Minister of a Caribbean island. She's been on television and radio to share her passion. All this in the space of 4 years. She is definitely a high achiever but you see it is possible.

Still think you can't do it? Well, there's a boy called Caleb Berkeley who can prove you wrong. At age 10, he is the published author and creator of "The Adventures of Moshe Monkey" series. He's authored 4 books already in the series and he has one more in the works for 2016. He may do one a book a year or so over the summer holidays. His books are beautifully illustrated and parents and children 5 to 12 love them. If he did only one book per year based on his growing ability, by the time he was 18 years he would be a published author of at least 11 books. They would all be generating income for him. There is also the benefit of putting that achievement on your college or university application.

Need one more boost? Well, there's a boy called Elisha Berkeley. He started his first book in May 2016. He's only 7 years old. By the time you read these words, his book will be published. He wanted to write a book since he was 5 years old but we told him he was too small. He was persistent and this year we saw his determination and encouraged him to go for it. It's not a big book but it is one that will give him an enormous sense of pride and a sense of accomplishment. Plus, he will be able to entertain a lot of children with his story. His book series is called "Mouzzie Mouse Adventures". Yes, he does plan to write more stories. I say sure, it beats a day job, any day of the week.

Still wondering if you can do it? Well, I have something to help you. Years ago, I actually developed a program called "Write Your Book in 90 Days." It was an online course designed to help walk any ordinary person through the process of writing their first book. It makes the whole process as easy as a piece of cake. I wanted it to be something that anyone can do and succeed even if they have low self-esteem. And the great thing is once you learn the process, it's just a matter of rinse and repeat to write other books. You can find this course online at http://berkeley.academy

Invent Something

If you haven't found your book, and you're not willing to teach, but, you are good with your hands and can sometimes be creative, then look for a problem, then invent the solution. Pray for some divine inspiration for the solution to the problem that you're trying to solve. Then, once you've solved it, get it patented and protected. I know one gentleman who invented an ingenious bookmark. Your invention may be inside of you.

Become An Artist

Maybe you can't invent something useful for humanity or your community. You can become an artist. Art has the capacity to touch the heart of another person. Caleb and I actually met a famous Columbian artist who now lives in Canada. We went to his gallery showing. His artworks were selling between $350 to $2500 dollars. And he makes his art out of recycled materials.

It was really interesting. He showed me one work that was made from an ironing board. I didn't even recognize it until he pointed it out. I love his creativity. His name is Mao Correa and his website is www.maocorrea.com. You should check it out and tell your friends to buy from him.

Art is something that adds character and energy to a home. And you might notice in the front section of the book, there is an art piece which was used as the cover for this book available for sale. If you're about Breaking the Poverty Curse then hang this artwork in your home or office as a reminder to you of your mission and vision. Let it motivate you. Grab the art at
http://cmberkeleymediagroup.com/shop

Start A Club/Society

This one takes more time to cultivate, but could generate larger long term returns on the time invested. You will have a group of like minded individuals connected to you. You can promote opportunities for vendors aligned with your society to showcase their materials for a fee. You can also sell your items to the group. Keep it lively and active in order to keep the people interested.

Today you can use technology to assist you in making the club a success. The website called www.meetup.com is one place where I was able to start a group for a small monthly fee. The site manages the automated meeting reminders, the rating of your meetings, the bulletin board and other features. It also promotes your meeting along with hundreds of other meetings, on its weekly email announcements.

Facebook has groups as well where you can communicate with members regularly and facebook groups are free to use. There are many new opportunities to use social media to harness the power of a club or society.

Become An Affiliate

If you don't have your own product or service at the moment, you can sell a product or service that another person has created in order to earn a commission. For example, many of the Multi-Level Marketing (MLM) models are based on that model. It's one way to earn an extra income. My issue with MLM is the ones that place mandatory buying on customers in order gain a benefit. You don't need a garage full of a company's stuff in order for you to make a commission. Online affiliate marketing has some great potential for people wanting to earn some extra cash.

You could refer people to one of our courses in BERKELEY ACADEMY. I've set up the academy to be able to do referral fees to people just like you. Because my personal philosophy is personal empowerment, I wanted my students to feel empowered to earn some cash for helping empower their friends too. Go to the website: **http://berkeley.academy/affiliate**

Become a Freelancer

Being a freelancer is changing of your mindset. You must expand your mind to the point where you think of short-term service, in exchange for remuneration. Think guerrilla service exchange. Get in, hit, and move on. This may not be the path you wish to remain on for your entire life, but it is a strategy for helping you get back on your feet. Working as a consultant, or for an agency. would be your option here. One website you can visit is www.elance.com for freelance jobs posted.

Start A Successful Blog

With the success of the internet and social media, it is now possible for people to begin making money at home from their blog. Got a particular hobby? Do you have a fetish that a lot of people might like (collect legos, love photos of toes, etc.) Start a blog to showcase your particular taste. In a world

276

of over 7 billion people, and more than 60% have access to the internet, you are sure to find people who like the same things you do. However, there is a particular process and system that must be followed in order to create a successful blog. It involves a lot of work. You have to work at your blog daily or weekly. Our academy has a course on how to get started on a successful blog at http://berkeley.academy

Start A Food Business

If cooking or preparing foods is your passion, they why not consider starting a food business. These days with technology and different techniques in outsourcing production, it is possible to create an entire food line of products if that is your desire. There is a person we know in Toronto. She started her little food business and would go out to different farmer's markets to sell her product. She also went to trade shows and other events where her product would be appreciated and purchased. She worked diligently while keeping her costs low. Recently I found out she makes over $150,000 per year on her little food business. That's quite a nice business given her humble start.

Start a Niche Business

So maybe you have no talent for cooking. Perhaps you could burn water if left unsupervised in the kitchen. Well perhaps you can consider starting a niche business in something you are really passionate about. The global community created via social media platforms now enable you to meet the world and tell the world about your particular niche product. In a world of 7 billion people, you're not the only one who loves your particular niche idea. Do some market research on whether it is in the market. Go for it.

Save and Save

We have just covered some ideas for generating cash flow. The next step is for you to keep more of what you make. In these severely constricted economic times, cash savings may

lose their value monthly, weekly or daily. You must still save.
This is important. But your savings must be in a cash
equivalent or something tangible.

Saving Co-op: I know of a method used among poor
people to save their money. There is no interest and it helps
people get the money when they need it. An example of how
this works is a group of 10 people come together and each
pay in $100 towards their goal. Each week one person gets
the $1000. People decide when they would like to be paid
the money. Those who need it earlier would get the money
earlier and still continue paying $100 each week. Those who

Week	1	2	3	4	5	6	7	8	9	10
Person 1	$1000	-100	-100	-100	-100	-100	-100	-100	-100	-100
Person 2	-100	$1000	-100	-100	-100	-100	-100	-100	-100	-100
Person 3	-100	-100	$1000	-100	-100	-100	-100	-100	-100	-100
Person 4	-100	-100	-100	$1000	-100	-100	-100	-100	-100	-100
Person 5	-100	-100	-100	-100	$1000	-100	-100	-100	-100	-100
Person 6	-100	-100	-100	-100	-100	$1000	-100	-100	-100	-100
Person 7	-100	-100	-100	-100	-100	-100	$1000	-100	-100	-100
Person 8	-100	-100	-100	-100	-100	-100	-100	$1000	-100	-100
Person 9	-100	-100	-100	-100	-100	-100	-100	-100	$1000	-100
Person 10	-100	-100	-100	-100	-100	-100	-100	-100	-100	$1000

need the money later would get the money towards the end.
This system of saving demands integrity among all the
savers. Since they are all relatively poor, this method helps
them meet their needs when it arises.

Person 1 might need the $1000 in week one for an important
bill and gets the money with the help of the other nine
people. The person collecting the cash in week 1 gets an
interest free loan of $900 from the others which is paid back
weekly until the last person is paid out. This helps those with
few financial options avoid credit card debt, interest fees,
service fees, and other costs and builds a saving habit.
Persons 2 to 10 all get an interest free loan of $900 as they
help someone in their group in need.

Note: This kind of saving mechanism is very informal and can only be done with persons of high integrity. Due to this level of informality and high integrity requirement, it is difficult for a selfish and untrusting person to participate in it.

The Gifting Circle (WARNING)

Years ago when the internet was still dialup I remember receiving a chain letter from someone. It had a list of about 10 names on the list with a few basic instructions. Basically I was to send $5 to each person on the list, then delete the first name, place my name on the bottom of the list and email it to all my friends with the same instructions. I remember looking at that and telling myself this is some scheme to take money from the gullible.

In 2017, I was told of an invite only "Gifting Circle." This gifting circle is actually a pyramid structure. There are 8 people at the base and one at the top. The people at the bast pay the person at the top $1000 each so the person at the top gets $8000 then is pushed off the pyramid. The pyramid then splits into 2 new pyramids which need to find 8 people for the base each. These 8 people will pay $1000 each to the person at the top. The enticement of this scheme is the lure of a quick $8000 for a small $1000 investment with no hard work involved. I explained to the lady who tried to introduce me to this that it seemed like a ponzi scheme. No actually money is created in this and the entire system depends on new money coming in via the base all the time in order to keep paying the person at the top.

Another flag for me was that the persons in the system all use code names so tracking each person is difficult.

There is no obligation for the person at the top to pay back into the system. They can take their money and run. Then it is everyone else below the top spot who has the pain of enticing a new "gifter" into this scheme. AVOID THIS!

The persons who run thus type of scheme target the poor and working poor who really need a "break." They try to sell the prospect of easily turning your small investment into BIG money overnight.

As a believer, you may have an opportunity like this presented to you. Don't be enticed into it. It is like lying in wait for innocent blood, in my opinion. Why do I say that? Because in order for you to get paid at the top, 8 innocent people need to be fleeced of their money. If you and your associates cannot find a total of 8 folks, you won't get paid.

This scheme is the result of what can happen when the method becomes corrupted by the ungodly preoccupation with greed. In a pyramid made up on 15 people, there can be only 1 winner and 14 losers hoping to recruit 14 other gullible folks in order that they might get a payday. Each of those 14 folks are now waiting and hoping for their $8,000 payday. Again, my warning is for believers to avoid this type of scheme.

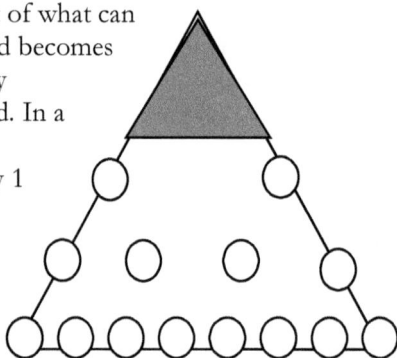

Beloved, however you choose to save, convert your paper into something valuable that can be stored over the long term, and won't lose value over time. And the item must be redeemable for cash if desired at a later date.

One raw chocolate author, speaker, and enthusiast, in one of his speeches mentioned that the raw cacao bean was used as both a currency and a food by an ancient culture. In the event they couldn't spend the bean, they would eat it and live.

This concept may be needed for these times. For those who can afford to stock up on dry foods, it will be more economical to buy in bulk and use it over time. Precious metals are also another way to save your money, but if you cannot afford that, then food is your option.

Try to save at least 30% or more of your earnings. Do this consistently and each time look for ways to increase the value of your earnings.

Give

Giving opens up a Spiritual doorway for good to come into your life. I'm not talking about giving to charities whose executive staff are on huge salaries. I also do not recommend giving to some TV-evangelist whose bank account is already overfull with millions, and who lives like a king in lavish and excesses. Giving in an insincere way to those who you know are misusing the money is not honouring your creator or truly spreading love in the world. It may even work in reverse causing a further contraction of your prosperity stream because you are enabling greater spiritual harm by your giving.
I'm talking about true, love-inspired giving to the poor and needy right in the neighbour where you live or work in.

2 Corinthians 9:7   Luke 10:29-37

Note the key points of each verse below:

_____

_____

_____

_____

This kind of giving is personal and purposeful. It is the kind recommended by the Bible for flowing blessings. You have to master this technique as another tool in your prosperity toolkit.

Set Goals and Persist

The mindset of a person who is goal oriented and who is willing to persist with a thing until the goal is achieved is what is also needed. If any person is given the keys to success but they are unwilling to persist then they will reap failure. You must never give up. If one road is blocked seek a reasonable detour. Remain focused!

Order the **Break The Poverty Curse Daily Success Workbook** seen on pg 10 to get started fast on this!

Here are some tips:
1. At the beginning of the month set 2-3 goals.
2. Work on them daily until achieved.
3. Review your progress each Sunday evening.
4. Begin each Monday morning with a plan for furthering your goals.
5. Repeat until your life is fulfilled.

Summary

This chapter has been a lot of information to consume. However, when you understand this, you can then proceed to gain more sources of revenue for yourself.

Here's a quick generic budget for your money.
30% - Save For Your Future
20% - Giving To People In Need
10% - Emergency Planning
40% - Day to Day living

If you create a budget now and you find that your percentages are way off, then you need to take steps to rectify the situation. You can cut back on your expenses and also increase your sources of revenue.

* * *

How can I do what IS GOOD AND RIGHT?

What man is he that desireth life, and loveth many days, that he may see good? **Keep thy tongue from evil**, and **thy lips from speaking guile. Depart from evil**, and <u>do good</u>; **seek peace**, and <u>pursue it.</u> The eyes of the LORD are upon the righteous, and his ears are open unto their cry.
~ Psalms 34:12-15

breakthepovertycurse.com

Breakthepovertycurse.com

Ancient Order of Prosperity

Being a property owner

Being without property

Being a vagrant/homeless

Being a debtor

Being a thief

Explained in our course at http://berkeley.academy

Course Note: In the course we mentioned more ways to make money quickly online. Write down 2 things you will work on in the next 30 days in the space above.

Write your notes from the course below.

_____

_____

_____

_____

_____

_____

_____

_____

_____

_____

_____

_____

_____

* * *

Stop And Think

Once again we stop and consider all the knowledge gained in this chapter. Examine your feelings.

Realization: I now understand that I need to have a plan to enable my prosperity, I see that the rules of the universe when understood and used properly can enable my prosperity in physical and spiritual endeavours. I am thankful for the new knowledge and the freedom from the CURSE it will usher in.

Prayer: Our Father in heaven, I am thankful for the knowledge I've gained here. Please guide me into the wise use of these concepts to achieve spiritual, physical and financial freedom from the CURSE. Bless my efforts as I step forward in gratitude and faith this day. Blessed be God(Yahuah) forever. Amen.

Affirmation: Today I will know myself and apply these concepts toward unlocking my prosperity.

* * *

Write Your Personal Insights Here

_____

_____

_____

_____

_____

_____

_____

_____

_____

_____

_____

_____

* * * * *

In our course on Breaking the Poverty Curse at Berkeley Academy, we tackle the topic in more details and give you more fast start money ideas for your cash flow situation. You are simply lacking in some core aspects of fast cash seeding and reaping. Check out the course at http://berkeley.academy/our-courses/

* * * * *

Vaughn Berkeley, MBA

The Resolution
Chapter 12

* * *

"Preacher man tell me heaven is under the earth. I know him
don't know what life is really worth" ~ Bob Marley (from
the song, Get Up, Stand Up!)

Choosing to become a person who takes action will have a
powerfully positive effect on your entire life. You gain
tremendously in all areas of your life when you make and
reach goals, when you do what you say you will do, when
you take care of things on time, and when others are
counting on you. You gain spiritually and materially. ~
Rabbi Zelig Pliskin

God(Yahuah) give me the freedom to shape the world
around me, to help others, and to finish the race honourably.
~ Vaughn Berkeley, MBA

* * *

The purpose of this chapter is to help you connect the dots
and put it all in perspective. Have you ever played the game
"Simon says", or gone on a scavenger hunt? In each of these
games the winner was the one who was able to follow
instructions and extend any advantage.

When the slaves were given their freedom some of them
rejected it because they had no idea what to do with it.
Freedom for the one rejecting it, meant a completely
unknown situation. It meant pain, suffering, possibly
hardship and even death. It meant breaking the prison of the
mind, which is the strongest prison built without human
hands.

A baby elephant is trained, by placing a chain around its leg
and tying that chain to a stump. When the baby elephant

tries to run it is stopped by the chain connected to the stump. However, when the elephant is grown only a simple rope handkerchief tied around the leg is sufficient to keep the elephant from running away. Why?

The mind of the elephant is trained to expect a strong chain around its leg and it never questions after that. So when the rope handkerchief is attached it does not question the difference in texture, colour or anything. Its programming tells it that it cannot move.

Sometimes human beings under the Poverty CURSE for a generation or more, like the adult elephant, forget to question the purpose of being, of life and of love.

Perhaps you've been trapped in the generational CURSE of poverty. Maybe your grandparents were poor and your parents were poor and now you are poor and all you see for your children is a future filled with poverty.

The Curse of Poverty Can End with You

The children of Israel had to go into the wilderness in order to escape the prison of slavery in Egypt. When the life seemed hard, some of them began to wish for the pleasures of Egypt. Some of their hearts were not totally converted to freedom.

Exodus 14:11-12   Exodus 4:3-4

Christ(Yahusha) voluntarily went into the wilderness for 40 days, in order to strengthen himself for the attacks of the enemy. Here's an ah-ha moment, the Curse of Poverty is the CURSE of SIN.

Ellen White (Confrontation, 1971) writes,
The halo of glory, which God had given holy Adam to cover him as a garment, departed from him after his transgression. The light of God's glory could not cover disobedience and sin. In the place of

health and plenitude of blessings, poverty, sickness, and suffering of
every type were to be the portion of the children of Adam…

Did you understand that? Our inheritance from Adam was
the suffering on earth created by his sin. However, we also
are at a point where we must overcome in the strength of
Him(Yahusha) that enables us to overcome. Christ(Yahusha)
has paid the bill in full. Victory can now be ours.

Who are you? A Man/Woman free from the CURSE!

Congratulations on coming this far in your personal journey
out of the Poverty CURSE. You have come this far, because
God(Yahuah) Himself desires your freedom, and you wanted
it for yourself.

Thus the partnership has been successful.

You got this far on your journey, because as you came upon
each obstacle that presented itself, you looked inside for the
divine strength to gain the victory. All of this was done even
though your knowledge of Him and His divine laws was
abstract.

Every little bit of knowledge gained was a piece of the puzzle
that showed your freedom. You also obediently acted on the
new knowledge. Freedom is your birthright.

The CURSE of Poverty is meant for those who reject this
freedom. Christ(Yahusha) is a Messiah for all peoples who
will accept Him. Divine laws govern universal bodies not
just earthly bodies. God(Yahuah) sent the prophet Jonah to
the people of Nineveh and they accepted the call to life. Will
you?

Exodus 14:11-12   Exodus 4:3-4

You are valuable! You are loved! You are worth the effort!
You are worth everything.

Here's a summary of what we learned together in this book:

1. We identified the core problem: The core problem is the CURSE of Poverty. Poverty is not only the lack of cash, but also ill health, low education, broken relationships and loss of hope and faith.
2. We did the self assessment: The self assessment highlighted the conditions which afflict the human form. We further narrowed these down to the ones most applicable to you. We looked at verses that seek to throw more light on the full ramification of these conditions.
3. We looked for real solutions: Your journey led you to the path of seeking solutions to the things that keep the CURSE of Poverty in your life.
4. We took action: Every checkpoint you visited was action. Every affirmation was the seed-thought for your prosperity action.

Love yourself because you are worthy of love. Love others because you love yourself.

Be a conduit for love and a source of love. Choose life. The CURSE is soon to be lifted. Just remember the warning that Jesus(Yahusha) told delivered folks: do not return to the past ways before a worst thing will befall you.

"Therefore take no thought, saying, What shall we eat? or, What shall we drink? or, Wherewithal shall we be clothed? (For after all these things do the Gentiles seek:) for your heavenly Father knoweth that ye have need of all these things. **But seek ye first the kingdom of God[Yahuah], and His righteousness; and all these things shall be added unto you.**" - Jesus (Yahusha), Matthew 6:31-33

* * *

Course Note: In the module, we talk about putting things together. This is the final exam in freedom from the POVERTY CURSE. Complete the network according to the instructions given in the course.

Write your notes from the course below.

_____

_____

_____

_____

_____

_____

_____

_____

_____

_____

_____

_____

_____

* * *

Stop And Think

Once again we stop and consider all the knowledge gained in this chapter. Examine your feelings.

Realization: I now understand that I need to have a plan to enable my prosperity, I see that the rules of the universe when understood and used properly can enable my prosperity in physical and spiritual endeavours. I am thankful for the new knowledge and the freedom from the CURSE it will usher in.

Prayer: Our Father in heaven, I am thankful for the knowledge I've gained here. Please guide me into the wise use of these concepts to achieve spiritual, physical and financial freedom from the Poverty CURSE. Bless my efforts as I step forward in gratitude and faith this day. Blessed be God(Yahuah) forever and ever. Amen.

Affirmation: Today I will know myself and apply these concepts toward unlocking my prosperity.

* * *

Write Your Personal Insights Here

_____

_____

_____

_____

_____

_____

_____

_____

_____

_____

_____

* * * * *

In our course on Breaking the Poverty Curse at Berkeley Academy, we tackle the topic in more details and give you more fast start money ideas for your cash flow situation. You are simply lacking in some core aspects of fast cash seeding and reaping. Check out the course at http://berkeley.academy/our-courses/

* * * * *

30-DAY Challenge

You have the book, now what? Do you do what the rest of the population does? Do you read the book, make some notes, say ah-ha a few times, and then do nothing?

In writing this book, my desire is for you to create a real change in your life. That's why I designed a 30-Day Challenge to accompany the book.

It was a 30-Day Challenge that got me started on Wordpress when I thought it was beneath me. Now I love wordpress.

This 30-Day email challenge is for the person who is self motivated but needs just a little bit of a push to stay on course over the next 30 days.

Link: http://breakthepovertycurse.com

* * * * *

30-DAY Email Coaching

Beloved, I have a burning desire on my heart to have people awaken out of the POVERTY Curse. You might say it is the passion that God has placed on me.

We have the complete course developed through our Berkeley Academy. As I was writing this book, I felt impressed to create a curriculum that can be delivered strictly via email. Hence the email coaching was born.

It is a curriculum designed to be emailed to you each day for 30 days. It takes you a few minutes to read each day and it helps you learn a heavenly concept for that day. It's the modern delivery mode for our modern society.

For now, I am only offering this 30-Day email coaching for those who buy the book package on my website. The value of this is that you are getting principles and precepts delivered to your inbox for 30 days. You can choose each day to do what is righteous.

In the future, I may decide to make it available for a stand alone price of $150 or more. But for now, you can get it when you purchase the appropriate book package on the site.

Link: http://breakthepovertycurse.com

* * * * *

Break The Poverty Curse Online Course

Course Description: The course is designed to help students understand the principles related to money and finances from a spiritual perspective. The course is based on the book by Vaughn Berkeley entitled, 'Break The Poverty Curse: Unlock Your Prosperity' The course also brings in additional material not available in the book but the extra knowledge can assist students in working toward their financial goals.

Who is this for? This course is for teenagers to adults who have a Christian background and would like to learn Biblical principles that God has put in place to help his children.

The course is offered online exclusively via the Berkeley Academy.

For course fees, registration requirements, and how to get started, go to Berkeley Academy at http://berkeley.academy

* * *

Berkeley Academy (http://berkeley.academy)
This is the online educational institute founded by Vaughn Berkeley and carrying on the tradition and heritage of the Berkeley name and role in educating the masses. Vaughn's passion has been education from as long as he can remember. The institute prides itself on providing non-conventional education to help people prepare a life of worth instead of prepare for a job.

* * * * *

About The Author

The POVERTY CURSE is the most effective path that leads to the slow but sure extinction of the victim. It tortures and imprisons its victim until all their hope is destroyed and they wish for death. ~ Vaughn Berkeley

Vaughn Berkeley, has a Masters of Business Administration (MBA) and Bachelor of Commerce degree. He is a life-long advocate for the poor. Being raised from humble beginnings himself, he has seen how crushing the power of the poverty CURSE can be. He saw his parents start successful businesses only to have them fail years later without any gains in life-style for his family.

Vaughn Berkeley is the President and CEO of CM Berkeley Media Group, Co-Publisher of Canada's Premier Holistic Lifestyle Magazine for the Vegan and Raw-Vegan Community, a Gansta Gardener on his block, and the author of several books.

Vaughn is also the creator of "The book on Quantum™" series of books. Whether you're looking for information on Quantum Personal Branding or Quantum Relationships,

Vaughn's got a Quantum book title for you. He will be collaborating with other authors in the future to bring more topics to his fans and readers.

Under Vaughn's Presidency at CESAR, he established a perpetual bursary system for the continuing education students of Ryerson University which has generated over $1 million dollars for students since its creation. Vaughn was the recipient of the Hugh Innis Award for Human Rights and Social Justice.

Vaughn's also a photographer and you may have seen some of his photos published in EternityWatch Magazine.

Vaughn's also a podcaster with his podcast entitled, "The Berkeley Life-Biz Podcast" The podcast is a source of practical information for living every life, contains interviews with ordinary people who are changing lives around them, and lots of nuggets of wisdom.

Vaughn is also a teacher at heart with a collection of online courses available via Berkeley Academy. These are courses aimed at helping people get access o life skills they would not find in traditional university or college environments.

If you know Vaughn by now, you'll see that he is a really humble guy who just wants to see people live better lives. This theme flows in whatever venture he is a part of.

It is his sincerest prayer for you that the words of this book will touch your heart and open your mind to getting out of the CURSE.

* * * * *

More from CM Berkeley Media Group

CM Berkeley Media Group, based in Canada, works with its authors to produce books which help to uplift the human spirit, spread the message of health and wellness, and offer practical insights in finances, and other areas. We also offer services to help authors convert their books to Kindle or ePUB format, get their book edited, and get a great cover design, and other services for independent authors.

Facebook Fan Page: cmberkeleymediagroup
Website: www.cmberkeleymediagroup.com
Email: info@cmberkeleymediagroup.com

Check out other great titles from our authors

For Adults

Eating4Eternity: Unlock Your Holistic Health Lifestyle.
Amazon Link >> http://amzn.to/1cO0kFd

Sweet Raw Desserts: Life Is Sweet Raw™
Amazon Link >> http://amzn.to/19msz2E

Can I Offer You A Cigarette: The Only Sure Way To Break The Smoking Habit
Amazon Link >> http://amzn.to/1enAfiJ

Colon By Design: Overcoming The Stigma Of Colon Sickness And Unlocking True Colon Health™
Amazon Link >> http://amzn.to/JGH05a

Fresh Food4Life™: The Case For Taking Back Control of Your Food And Empowering Your Family And Community.
Amazon Link >> http://amzn.to/J9yrQF

Break The Poverty Curse: Unlock Your Prosperity 2017

For Teens and Young Adults

The Youth Leadership Empowerment System™
Try out the FREE mini-course for youth.
Amazon Link >> http://amzn.to/1hRtMPy

For Children

The Adventures of Moshe Monkey and Elias Froggy: A
Healthy Business (Book 1)
Amazon Link >> http://amzn.to/1QU7hxF

Moshe and Elias Build A Garden (The Adventures of Moshe
Monkey and Elias Froggy) (Book 2)
Amazon Link >> http://amzn.to/1mI53Vn

Moshe and Elias Tropical Vacation (The Adventures of
Moshe Monkey and Elias Froggy) (Book 3)
Amazon Link >> http://amzn.to/1mI4Amd

Living Foods for Boys and Girls (The Adventures of Moshe
Monkey and Elias Froggy Book 4)
Amazon Link >> http://amzn.to/1QU6DQS

Mouzzie Mouse Adventures: Mouzzie Goes Home (Book 1)
Check for it on Amazon.com

For more great info from the author, fun activities for your
children, and more, visit: http://mosheandelias.com

* * * * *

Want to become a published author in 90 days? CM Berkeley
Media Group has an online training program to help anyone
aspiring to achieve this dream. Find out more about it and
realize your dream at
http://cmberkeleymediagroup.com/writeyourbookin90d
ays/

Great Resources

The Book on Quantum Website
www.thebookonquantum.com
This is the website to find all the information on current books and upcoming books in the series, "The Book on Quantum", by Vaughn Berkeley.

88Deals4U.com
This website is a great website for people looking for deals on items they use everyday. When you're on a budget and need to save money, then this is the online website for you.

EternityWatch Magazine
(www.eternitywatchmagazine.com)
EternityWatch Magazine is the premier magazine for those seeking a truly holistic approach to health and wellness. The magazine is founded on the belief that good health is everyone's birthright and that by proper education, people can make the right choices to maintain their good health. The magazine is focused on plant-based nutrition, thus it caters to the rapidly growing vegan, and raw/living foods movement. You can get it free online just by signing up for it.

Eating4Eternity.org (www.eating4eternity.org)
Eating4Eternity is founded by Jenny Berkeley and is focused on her personal coaching approach. On the site, you will find news articles on health and wellness, Jenny's blog posts with her personal insights into what is happening in the medical field, paid courses and webinars, and some free information.

FreshFood4Life.com (www.freshfood4life.com)
Fresh food for life is part of living a healthy life. This website has information about a revolutionary garden solution for the home owner with no space. You can view videos, articles and order your own garden system. You can grow 24 crops in you very own kitchen. I have one of these and so can you.

**Hippocrates Health Institute
(www.hippocratesinst.org)**
Hippocrates Health Institute is the premier institute for alternative health and wellness. With over 50 years of experience in educating people to take control of their health destiny, the institute has a solid foundation. Their website talks about their programs, plus you can find copies of their magazine.

**CM Berkeley Media Group
(www.cmberkeleymediagroup.com)**
CM Berkeley Media Group is the digital media company founded by Vaughn Berkeley. The company publishes books that have a message to uplift individuals. There are books for children, teens, and adults. You can also purchase resources from the authors online via the website.

Berkeley Academy (http://berkeley.academy)
This is the online educational institute founded by Vaughn Berkeley and carrying on the tradition and heritage of the Berkeley name and role in educating the masses. Vaughn's passion has been education from as long as he can remember. The institute prides itself on providing non-conventional education to help people prepare a life of worth instead of prepare for a job.

* * * * *

For Your Personal Notes

www.ingramcontent.com/pod-product-compliance
Lightning Source LLC
LaVergne TN
LVHW051224080426
835513LV00016B/1393